Making Space for the Spirit

Making Space for the Spirit

Developing a Contemplative Christian Retreat Center

A Personal Reflection by
Jennifer Kerr Graves

Foreword by
Kathi Bentall

RESOURCE *Publications* · Eugene, Oregon

MAKING SPACE FOR THE SPIRIT
Developing a Contemplative Christian Retreat Center

Resource Publications
An Imprint of Wipf and Stock Publishers
199 W. 8th Ave., Suite 3
Eugene, OR 97401

www.wipfandstock.com

PAPERBACK ISBN: 978-1-4982-2075-0
HARDCOVER ISBN: 978-1-4982-2077-4

Manufactured in the U.S.A.

Photographs copyright by Cherie Westmoreland.

*Dedicated to the Volunteer Core Community in recognition
and appreciation of their loving service*

Contents

Foreword

I stood on top of Cates Hill on Bowen Island for the first time in early 2001. My parents, Howard and Shirley Bentall, had invited me to participate with them in the creation of a retreat center, and we were viewing the potential site. I commented that it was beautiful but not the place for a retreat center. But despite my initial dismissal, the three of us, along with many others, embarked that day on a Spirit led unfolding that would result in the creation of Rivendell Retreat Center on Cates Hill. The story of this unfolding is described beautifully in the pages that follow.

But, when the story started, the way was not always clear and the path not always a straight line. In many ways, it was like traveling through a labyrinth. For over 4000 years, people have walked the labyrinth as a form of spiritual pilgrimage. Every walker follows a circuitous path to reach the center, the place of illumination, and then returns the same way back out to the world.

To walk a labyrinth, you must choose to begin the journey by entering into the path before you. My parents were in their elder years when the opportunity to create a retreat center appeared. They were clear that they wanted to do this, despite questions about their age and sanity at undertaking such a large project. They could not be dissuaded. So they stepped forward, following an inner knowing, and began their journey.

The shape of a labyrinth cannot be seen by the person walking within it. Only distance can bring the perspective needed to view the whole. My father provided that frame of reference for those of us mired in the details. My mother and I were busy creating legal organizations, visioning meetings and making the myriad of intricate decisions needed in a project of this size. But my father's experience as a Baptist minister and leader in the church enabled him to keep hold of the broader vision. At 84 years old when we began, he became our constant voice of encouragement and faith in what was being birthed. He was generally quiet, yet amazingly attentive in all our visioning meetings. When he did speak, usually with a few well chosen words, what he said caught our attention and kept us on track.

A labyrinth also requires attention to detail, not only in the walking but also in the construction. We built a labyrinth on municipal land near Rivendell in time for our 5th anniversary. The project was very labor intensive, using large stones which had to be chosen carefully and fitted together. My mother's loving meticulousness was like that path. The lodge at Rivendell has her touch throughout the building, from the diligently selected furniture to the coasters. She poured herself into the challenge of creating a fully functioning retreat center, bringing it to fruition in just 18 months. She died 3 years after Rivendell was finished, but up to the week before she passed, she was still writing checks and keeping up her hand written ledger of accounts. She took much delight and deep satisfaction in seeing the dream come to life.

Any pilgrim who walks the labyrinth path is faced with surprise turns. You think you are heading one way, and then the path turns in an unexpected direction. My initial vision for a retreat center included small hermitage cabins for more solitude, but this was not appropriate for the top of Cates Hill. Over time, the plan grew and shifted to one of a retreat center in two locations, and we now have a hermitage property offering the solitude I had envisioned. We had also originally thought we would need to follow the conventional model of a caretaker couple to run the center, but this gave way to the more radical model of a volunteer community of mostly retirees to host the incoming groups and individuals. Shortly after we opened, a most delightful surprise came when

Marks and Margaret McAvity reversed their initial decision and decided to become community members for a three month trial period. Thirteen years later, they continue to be an essential part of the life and spirit of Rivendell, and they, along with the other community members, have formed the web that continues to hold Rivendell and our principles.

As you journey towards the center of the labyrinth, the path often takes you quite close to the place of illumination then veers away. There were and continue to be moments when we come close to glimpsing the mystery behind Rivendell. Even at the start, the convergence of three distinct paths, was an example. The developer, Wolfgang Duntz had a vision for a retreat center, he connected with my parents who desired to create a meaningful legacy, and that dovetailed with my own experience leading retreats. We only needed to yield to the different threads that were coming together. There were dreams that encouraged us, messages that helped to dissipate rising tensions, and people who appeared just as we needed them. And even now, as our community is aging and in need of more members, I remind myself to trust that those who are right for Rivendell will be beckoned.

Finally, there have been moments of awe and illumination, like those you find at the labyrinth's center. Those moments are more than can be counted. They include the opening of Rivendell in June 2002, 18 months after the journey started, as we gathered around a large water filled clay pot and placed floating candles that represented our prayers of blessing for this place. About 2 years later, I led a silent retreat for people from Vancouver's Downtown Eastside, and as the group ate in silence, I sensed a timelessness and deep gratitude for the accessibility of Rivendell. I knew that "it was good." In the last few years of my father's life, those who came to Rivendell could witness the sacred moment each day when my father, bent over with age yet standing tall, would grab the rope to ring the bell for our daily 5:00 prayer.

As I look back on those years, I am awed by the privilege of working so closely with my parents. While they remained true to their Baptist roots and expression of their faith, they continued to grow and were open to different ways of approaching the spiritual journey. Even the labyrinth was a stretch for both of them, but when we roughly drew one in the parking lot, they were willing to try walking it. They embodied the challenge each of us face to embrace those who experience their spiritual journey in a different way to our own. This spirit of openness has become an essential part of Rivendell's way of being.

As Rivendell was unfolding and growing, people often commented that this story needed to be written. I knew that I would not be able to take on that task. It is not my gift. Once again, the right person came along. While Jenn Graves and I worked towards the creation of the second retreat site with small hermitage cabins, we often talked about the uniqueness of Rivendell. What follows is her description of the unfolding. Like my father, her viewpoint provides a different perspective. Although she was not involved in the beginnings of Rivendell, through her gift of attentive listening, she has been able to beautifully weave together the story of Rivendell. I am deeply grateful to her for her willingness to give hours of her time, to pour over the notes from our meetings, and to interview all of us involved. Her spirit of generosity reflects the same graciousness that created Rivendell. Our hope is that this book will in some way inspire you to follow the visions that arise in your own hearts, to take that step into the labyrinth of your own spiritual journey.

Kathi Bentall

Preface

This book is a faithful, reflective telling of the development of one type of contemplative Christian retreat center. While there are many different types of Christian Retreat centers, this one is run by a volunteer hosting community, does not offer retreat programs for people to sign up for, and welcomes from people from all socio-economic backgrounds because of its radically justice promoting principle of accessibility.

My desire to write this story began when I began working with Kathi Bentall, one of the founders of The Rivendell Lodge on Cates' Hill, to develop the Rivendell Hermitage[1]. Since my undergraduate days I have held a vision of a retreat center where people could pull away from all the busyness and demands of everyday life and meet God face to face. I needed this space myself. Nearly every day I withdrew from the social demands of dorm life for an hour on my own to walk the back 40. I took with me my jacket to sit on, my journal, and occasionally my Bible or other book. I have discovered that in every stage of life I have needed this space and that loved ones, friends, co-workers, neighbors, even talkative strangers who share their stories while they share my bus ride, also long to find space for their own spiritual refreshment, renewal, and growth.

---

1. The Hermitage is the originally envisioned development of a second Rivendell site with a focus on individuals and solitude.

I envisioned this retreat space as inclusive, accessible, and unstructured, welcoming people on the margins as well as the mainstream of the church and society. I did not know of any such place but I envisioned this as a way for people to seek spiritually even if they would not set foot in the church. I wrote down my vision and saved it.

Several years later I met Kathi Bentall when she was my supervisor for a ministry placement. We soon discovered we shared a similar vision for retreat. This vision is slowly becoming a reality. A developer donated the land, a foundation donated the cost of the main building, and we were finally ready to begin developing the very retreat center we had dreamed about years before. It was a very exciting time. Until I realized that I did not know the first thing about starting a retreat center. I realized I was in way over my head. Thus began my reading and research.

I began by reading the book, "Poustinia: Christian Spirituality of the East for Western Man," by Catherine de Hueck Doherty; a short, unpublished reflection called, "I Run in the Dark," about the development of the Nestucca Retreat Center (now closed); and a likewise unpublished story about the origins and development of The Desert House of Prayer, a retreat center in Arizona. I also delved deep into the writings of St. Theresa of Avila (founder of many monastic communities). While this gave me a starting place, I also wanted to know more about Rivendell's particular history as it related to the development of the Hermitage.

So with this hope I began gathering information about Rivendell's beginnings. I read Shirley Bentall's unpublished journal and the meeting minutes of the steering committee. I then met with Wolfgang Duntz, Kathi Bentall, and Rivendell Lodge's founding hosts, to hear Rivendell's oral history. I felt like the luckiest fly on the wall; peering back into those early days when Rivendell was born. I kept thinking, "these are the stories that make us who we are": stories of risk, hard work, long journeys, and finally, success. I heard of hope long held before it was fulfilled and I thought of my own struggles, failures, and shortfalls. These stories taught me the importance of being guided by vision and inspired me to persevere.

As I wrote this story I began to hear of other retreat centers closing, primarily from lack of funds or unsustainable hosting communities. Hearing of centers closed in spite of a need for them, I realized that Rivendell's success is worth learning from and remembering. So join me as we listen in on Rivendell's stories, hearing how they held, realized, and sustained their vision to make space for the Spirit, inspiring us to do the same. And so I would like to share with you the story of the Rivendell Retreat Center.

Introduction

This is an amazing story—quite unexpected and hopeful. But before I begin I want you to know, if you don't already, what Rivendell Retreat Center is and why this story is important, particularly right now. Rivendell Retreat Center is a Christian spiritual retreat center located at the top of Cates Hill, on Bowen Island, in British Columbia, Canada. It has a year round occupancy rate of around 90%, nearly unheard of in the hospitality industry. Nearly 3,000 retreatants stay at the retreat center each year, many of whom hope to hear its story when they come. Telling this story is more important, however, than simply satisfying curiosity.

Right now, retreat centers are closing around the world because they have become unsustainable. As the communities that hold these sacred spaces age and die they are not being replaced by a younger generation. Catholic retreat centers which offered minimal structure and financially accessible retreat space are being shut down and sold as the nuns and priests who host them can no longer maintain the buildings nor have the energy to host. There are Protestant retreat centers, but these are generally expensive and run on a very different model, based on offering programs rather than gently structured space for rest and spiritual renewal. Rivendell Retreat Center differs from both these models. Rivendell Retreat Center is so unique that it is difficult to explain exactly what it is like to those who have not experienced it for themselves. Most people are familiar with retreat centers that offer guided retreats and a variety of programs, so to explain Rivendell's unique vision of simply providing space is difficult.

Rivendell is, first and foremost, a place. It is built in a quiet, picturesque rural area that is both away from the city and yet near enough to get to easily. It consists of one lodge, one cottage, one sanctuary, one woodshed, and many trails lacing the hillside. Then, it is considered a sacred space. It does not only have a sanctuary, it is one. The building called the sanctuary only holds and symbolizes the innermost life and intention of the rest of the place. The entire place, paths and all, is a sanctuary—a holy place of safety where people can encounter God in quiet so they can recognize God with them in the noise as well. Thirdly, it is rooted in the person of Jesus and the traditions of the historic Christian community that have characterized monastic communities throughout the ages. Finally, with radical originality, Rivendell is hosted by volunteers and is accessible to all who seek what Rivendell offers, including those with limited resources and special needs.

This is the only center I have heard of that operates with these principles. It is one of the most wonderful and unique things about Rivendell: that all the hosts are volunteers and that those who pay five dollars a night are welcomed as warmly as those who pay a hundred, so long as they are paying "generously within what they can afford." In this way Rivendell Retreat Center becomes a place of social as well as spiritual transformation.

Although Protestant in its roots, it offers minimally structured space, rather than programs, hosted primarily by an elder community that was characteristic of some Catholic retreat centers, and holds a principle of financial accessibility. It continues to thrive well into its second decade. In order to do so, it is finding creative ways to address the unique challenges that come from this model. It must be diligent to communicate clearly the vision and purposes of Rivendell to potential retreatants who are considering coming on this kind of retreat for the first time. The hosting community must work with groups and individuals to protect the ambiance and focus on spaciousness to attend to the inner, contemplative life by encouraging retreatants to make room in their retreat for the spaciousness of the contemplative life and requiring groups to make space for this through minimal programming. It must hold the life of Rivendell through practices of prayer that undergird and permeate every aspect of the generous hospitality for which it is known. It must support its aging community in a sustainable way. And finally, it must continue to consider new ways to uphold and renew its radical vision of social justice through its principle of accessibility.

For well over ten years now, this little place tucked on the hilltop of a small island suburb, continues to thrive, able to continue to offer its radical welcome while many centers without such an accessibility principle, are closing their doors and being sold. Throughout Rivendell's story the people involved have acted in unexpected and Christ centered ways. They have given generously of their possessions, their money, their lives, and their experiences, motivated by what is unseen, rather than what is seen, to make the vision of this unique, accessible model of spiritual retreat a successful, sustainable, reality.

Acknowledgements

T his book has been a community project and it would not have reached its final finished form without the many gifts of the community of people who have made it possible. First I want to thank all the people who loving and patiently shared their memories and stories with me, bringing this story into my life and heart.

I want to thank all the members of the Core Community. They have all given many hours to share their experiences and insights with me and I am grateful. Thanks to everyone for sharing their memories. I am sorry that they did not all make their way into this telling and only wish I could include all of which you so generously shared. Thank-you also for the guidance you gave that helped keep the story both accurate and alive.

Thank-you to Wolfgang Duntz for shifting my trajectory from "textbook" to "mystery."

In particular I want to thank John and Wendy Hardy who, by coincidence, hosted me nearly every time I stayed at Rivendell to write. You were wonderful hosts whose contagious enthusiasm made it into this story in all sorts of backdoor ways. Thank you for showing me the wooden cross, carved from a single piece of wood that was an inspiration to me as I wrote and for your gift of blessing I sat under as I persevered through the writing process.

Thanks to Margaret McAvity for your insight into the challenges and blessings of retreat work, your memories of Howard Bentall, your magical ability to pull whatever you need from your magic closet (especially the poem, "The Woodcarver"), and the time you spent with Kathi and me, checking the accuracy of what I wrote and looking through pictures with me.

Thank-you to Cherie Westmoreland who put much loving reflection, artistry, and time into the photographs that give a visual glimpse into the heart and place of Rivendell. All the photos except for images 2 and 4 were taken by Cherie.

Thank-you especially to Kathi for more things than I can take time to innumerate here. In particular, thank-you for your guidance throughout this project, your gentle encouragement, your patience, and your gift of vision holding.

Thanks also to the two wordsmiths I discovered among Rivendell's hosts: Barb Rendell and Marilyn Gullison. Thank-you Barb for your lovely way with words and the picturesque phrases you spin—many of them have found their way into this telling. And thank you Marilyn for helping me stay concise. Thank you to Tim Scorer and Graham Schultz for their work editing the final product.

Last but not least, thank-you to my family: Dave, Melissa, and Alexis for their loving support, their feedback, their participation, and all the time they have given me to work on this story and pursue the visions of my heart.

This? It's a story.
I think, if you would analyze most sacred places:
monasteries, churches, retreats,
any places which have some kind of a soul to them,
you will not find deliberate planning.
Maybe to carry it out there was some
deliberate planning necessary,
But the idea was formed out of a story,
out of a dream,
out of an urge,
out of something bigger than ourselves.

Wolfgang Duntz

I.

Holding the Vision

Napkin Drawings

This story, the story of how a unique place like Rivendell Retreat Center came to be, begins with a mystery. It is the mystery of countercultural generosity: a developer plans to donate six and a half acres of prime real estate to people he barely knows and two people who had just received a long-awaited inheritance consider how they can give it away. And somehow these people find each other at just the right moment to bring forth their commonly held vision of spiritual renewal, hospitality, and accessibility: a year-round retreat for whomever may need it, whether or not they have the means to pay for it. It is a story, a story birthed from generosity and vision.

Wolfgang Duntz was the developer with a vision and a site. As I sat with him across his desk, in his small bright office in Snug Cove, I was moved by his longing for places of safety and unconditional acceptance where people could ask existential questions and seek spiritual renewal. As he was developing the rugged, treed hillside of Cates Hill into a small and inviting residential community, he envisioned a retreat center for precisely this purpose. He had the top seven acres zoned for retreat but ten years later Wolfgang's vision was still unrealized.

Throughout this decade he had actively sought people who claimed to share his dream. He met people and listened to stories and dreams, hoping that one of them would hold a vision and values similar to his own. Many people came forward, but none were what he called the "right fit." Wolfgang finally sought out a local theological college. He and his business manager, Larry Adams, met with their board and and offered them the dedicated land if they would build an inclusive retreat center for spiritual renewal. They turned down his offer.

Wolfgang and Larry shared their disappointment as they drove home, neither knowing that one heart continued to burn with the vision of retreat Wolfgang had presented. One man, Paul Stevens, had not joined the rest in turning down Wolfgang's offer. His heart and his mind were sparked by Wolfgang's dream and later that night he talked about it with his friend Ken Smith. Then, while this dream was still fresh in his thoughts, Ken went out for lunch with some other friends and he passed on this story over lunch. The story of man with a dream of retreat and the land to realize it.

Howard and Shirley Bentall, both of whom had passed away by the time I arrived at Rivendell, had recently come into a family inheritance and were still trying to decide how they wanted to use the money. I read in Shirley's journal that on October 6th, the day after Paul and Ken's conversation, Howard and Shirley went out for lunch with their friend, this same Ken Smith, and his wife Ruth. Howard was 87 years old and Shirley, thirteen years his junior, was 74. Although they had already spent or designated much of their inheritance by starting up Kinbrace and the Salsbury Community Houses[1], they also had another type of community they wanted to realize: a community of retreat.

Their daughter, Kathi, who I met through her work at the Listening Post[2], had been going on retreats for several years. She had

---

1. Kinbrace is a home for refugee claimants to live when they first come to Canada and the Salsbury Community Houses offer affordable community housing to those who may not otherwise be able to obtain it. Both were initiatives arising from Grandview Calvary Baptist Church.

2. The Listening Post is an inner city space for silence and spiritual listening that was co-founded by Kathi Bentall and the late Lorraine Lamarre of the Sisters of St. Anne. It has functioned successfully since 2000 staffed solely by volunteers.

received training in spiritual direction and had begun to lead regular retreats with residents of Vancouver's Downtown Eastside. I am sure that Howard and Shirley had witnessed their daughter's increasing involvement for they knew that she too held a vision of a retreat center. Kathi's present involvement, her mother's lifetime experience leading retreats for women, and their mutual, lifelong desire to create communities for renewal, fit perfectly with Wolfgang's vision, shared as they joined a friend for a simple luncheon date.

After the lunch with Ken and Ruth, Shirley went home and began a new list: "Significant Dates re: a Retreat Center on Bowen Island." She notes "October 6, 2000: lunch with Ken and Ruth Smith at the White Spot (Park Royal) where Ken mentioned the property available for a retreat center on Bowen Island." This is the only notation that we have about this meeting where the streams of vision came together for the first time. But perhaps it is here, in this West Vancouver restaurant, that Shirley made her "drawings on a napkin,"[3] her first tentative conceptions of the retreat building and community that has come to be known as Rivendell.

These coinciding stories are all like drawings on napkins: Wolfgang's vision and the steps he took to preserve it, Paul's burning heart that retained the dream his fellow board members had rejected, Kathi's increasing awareness of and involvement with retreats as a form of spiritual renewal, and the lunch with Howard and Shirley when Ken mentions Wolfgang's property and vision. They were all rough and unrealized, not yet characterized by deliberate planning, but full of possibility and hope in a story greater than themselves.

3. Thank-you to Barb Rendell for introducing me to this delightful phrase when telling me about these early visioning days.

II.

Realizing the Vision

Drawings Enfleshed:
Design and Development

The conversation over lunch with Ken and Ruth Smith had opened the door of an idea in Howard and Shirley's minds. On December 1st when they held a dessert party, Ken came bringing with him slides: pictures of Cates Hill taken by Paul Stevens. They now saw the dream in its context: a real place of trees and hilltops, rocky outcrops and ocean views. I imagine these images filled their thoughts through Advent and Christmas. Shirley recorded in her diary that on the 9th of January, 2001 she phoned Paul for the developer's name and phone number and on the 10th she arranged a time to meet that developer, Wolfgang, and see Cates Hill.

On the day Wolfgang received Shirley's phone call he had nearly given up hope that he would ever find the right partners for his project:

> Out of nothing; I remember it. I was somewhere out in the field, as usual very hectic. I got a call from Larry: "there is a couple here, they have been up at the site, 'the pinnacle' we called it, and they want to talk to you about it." And having met so many frauds, or let's say flakes, I said, "you know Larry, I am very busy, they have to wait like anybody else." When I came back to the office there was a little pink slip, "Howard and Shirley Bentall want

to meet with you," (The name Bentall meant nothing to me). So I called them and we met a few days later.[1]

On January 15th Shirley and Howard boarded the 12:05 ferry bound for Snug Cove, Bowen Island and met Wolfgang for the first time at 1:30pm to tour the peak of Cates Hill. Shirley's journal is factual, organized and not given to many outbursts of emotional expression, so when I read her short entry on January 15, I nearly laughed at the contrast which showed her enthusiasm: "*Our first visit to Cates Hill!* (italics, underline, and exclamation mark are all hers). The napkin drawings were becoming an unfolding journey, an adventure into reality.

The realization of Rivendell was no simpler in its development than it was in the coming together of all the major players. As I listened to the founding stories and read the minutes of the steering committee and Shirley's journal, I noticed three main strands of development woven together to create the retreat community and buildings. I have named these: 1) the creation of financial and legal structures, 2) building the lodge and cottage, and 3) community formation. Rivendell's founders had to attend simultaneously to the many tasks of all three strands in order to welcome her first retreatants on June 2, 2002.

While preparations for building construction were underway, plans drawn up and approved, roads thought of and made, construction team assembled and the ground blasted and prepared, they also addressed the financial and legal requirements of development. They applied for building permits and land transfers and waited to see if they were approved; they made decisions about who pays for what and when; and Shirley, Wolfgang, and Kathi were hard at work figuring out the best way to facilitate the donations and the vision. They created a charitable foundation and society, working with lawyers, lawyers, and more lawyers to help with all the decisions and applications. Shirley writes in her notes more than once: "*another* lawyer" (her italics).

1. Wolfgang Duntz.

A name, too had to be thought of; Wolfgang came through on this one. But would the name be available so they could use it? More legal work and the name was approved: Rivendell it is! Office visits to work on legal and financial details played tag with visits out to the site to see how construction is going. Four days after seeing Cates Hill,[2] Shirley, Howard, and Kathi met with Wolfgang and Dennis Dallas, who would become the construction manager for the Rivendell development. Then, for two weeks Shirley and Kathi worked on forming their visions for the retreat center[3].

Up until now it had seemed that everyone was on the same page. Shared values and shared intent should have meant shared vision details, yet when they brought their written work together, Kathi's vision and her mother's vision seemed to differ greatly. What should they do? Kathi asked her friend Rita to read what she and her mother had written and give her opinion. Rita read both visions and saw that the differences were not in vision but focus. Together, Shirley's focus on groups and Kathi's focus on individuals had developed into a vision of one retreat center with two different locations; one for groups and one for individuals. Kathi and Shirley then came up with a new vision statement to reflect the two-site retreat vision.

Wolfgang liked the idea of the two-site retreat center and immediately began to consider how to participate in this new development. On Valentine's Day Kathi saw the Cates Hill property, the site of the Lodge, for the first time. Two weeks later Wolfgang took Kathi, her parents, and her brother and his wife, over to a property in Cowan Point that Wolfgang already had in mind for the second site[4].

Now planning began in earnest, following a three phase development process outlined in Shirley's notes: *First Phase*: 1. Prepare sketches and plans for the first site, with cost estimates and time frame; 2. Figure out all the financial, legal, and organizational aspects necessary to ensure the completion of the current

2. January 19, 2001.
3. February 2-12, 2001.
4. February 26, 2001.

development and its ongoing sustainability; 3. Select an appropriate second site. *Second Phase*: Cates Hill. *Third Phase*: Second Site.

Everything went like clockwork during Phase One and within weeks the Rivendell Foundation and the Rivendell Society[5] were formed, the sketches and plans for the retreat center on Cates Hill were completed and they were ready to move into the second phase which was concerned with the its construction, community, and operations.

A Little Architectural Aside

Through many personal stories people shared about Shirley, I soon came to appreciate that Shirley Franklyn Bentall was known for her dedication to details. No detail, however small, seemed beneath her notice. I heard that during construction, as she walked through the building she amazed her tour guides by noticing every change that

5. The Rivendell Foundation is the legal charitable funding organization and owner, the Rivendell Society is the legal charitable operating society.

had been made. Not surprisingly, Shirley approached the visioning of Rivendell's building with this same attention to detail.

When Shirley met with Wolfgang and Dennis for their first talk about the layout of the building, she somewhat tentatively pulled out of her large black handbag an 8 1/2 by 11 inch piece of paper. On it was a pencilled draft of how she thought the building should look. Now, Wolfgang and Dennis had often seen "lay people" pull such drawings out of pocket or purse and they were prepared to look at her ideas with the polite condescension that "those who know" offer to "those who don't know." What they saw floored them. Apparently, so the stories say, Shirley's drawings were perfect to a detail. When Wolfgang handed them to Dennis, who was himself a gifted designer, he said "This is perfect." When Don Nicholson, the architect, looked them over he said he could not improve upon her design. Don took her drawings seriously, gave them depth and dimension and created the face of Rivendell that we are familiar with today.

Construction Days

Now the construction of Rivendell began, led by Dennis. Although I thought it sounded like a pretty ideal development, the project was not without an occasional problem, which I appreciated— these somehow rescued the story from the encroaching feeling of unreality.

One of the battles that had to be faced was with the public health authorities about the kitchen facility. Kathi and Shirley knew that in order to make Rivendell financially accessible the lodge could not have a staffed kitchen. Staffing a kitchen would increase operating costs so greatly that groups and individuals with limited means would not be able to afford to come. Kathi had learned this through her experience looking for retreat places where they could cook their own food and so offer affordable retreats for those in the inner city. A facility the size of the lodge generally requires a commercial kitchen. Wolfgang and Shirley, however, took on the challenge and made a presentation to the appropriate governing body. Miraculously with some changes to the design they were given permission to create the unstaffed, non-commercial kitchen they hoped for. This has proven to be an essential aspect to the principle of accessibility.

Very late in the construction another problem arose. As the large gathering room, *Grandview*, was being completed, Shirley walked through the site and looked in on it. As soon as she saw the room she realized with dismay that the room dimensions she had planned were not nearly big enough. She mentioned aloud her regret that the room would not hold twenty-five people as she had intended. She did not, however, suggest that any changes be made to the room this late in its construction.

That night Dennis stayed late at the site. The next day when Shirley walked through the site again Dennis had knocked out the original back wall and extended it several feet. He had designed the new outer wall to contain many windows along the sides and the back thus creating a much larger room: bright and open with a beautiful view. Shirley was amazed and grateful for Dennis' generous initiative and building improvement. Dennis's gift of this space continues to be appreciated by the many retreat groups who use that room. If you want to see the difference for yourself, when you go into the Grandview Room, take a look where the wall seems to jut into the sides of the room at its center depth. These pillars mark the original placement of the back wall.

Despite these minor set backs, Wolfgang remembers Rivendell's construction with the surprise and awe of the mysterious,

> In 40+ years of construction I have never seen a construction project like that. There was no stress, which is unheard of for a construction project. Also, I have never heard of it and I would be surprised if there was, ever a harsh word. The [workers] wouldn't go home after work, [instead] they were hanging out. They had a fire, they drank their beers, but it was a continuous loving, so [there was] never . . . any disharmony.

Of the many available stories, there are two more that I think best reveal the spirit of those early development days. One goes back to Rivendell construction days and the other is a note of "graffiti" that was written on Rivendell's cement slabs before fireplace stone work concealed it.

Several years after Rivendell's construction a young man walked into the Rivendell office. This young man had helped to build the Rivendell cottage. Although this was several years after the completion of the retreat center he still told stories of the fun that the construction crew had while building it.[6] This young man had brought his girlfriend with him and he wanted to know if they could go through the cottage at Rivendell so that he could show her this project, "so maybe we could build one for ourselves, just like it!" His pride was evident.

I also found these words in a photograph of an unfinished fireplace in the Rivendell construction site: On the unfinished wall of rough grey concrete blocks, in a bold scrawl under the inscriber's name is the statement: "2001-2002—*Lot of Fun and A Lot to Do!*"

---

6. Thank-you Wendy Hardy for sharing this story.

As the outer structure came together all the interior details also need attention: interior decoration, furniture, bedding, plates, bathroom fixtures, the kitchen, blinds, and flooring. Millions of little details inside and out that went into the building that are still noticed, thanks to Shirley's eye for details. Ten years after the Lodge opened its doors, people who knew Shirley said, "her imprint is everywhere on this place." Shirley picked out many of the furnishings herself and everything, from lamps to linens, coasters and cushions were stored in Shirley and Howard's garage until Rivendell was ready for them.

The building was ready just in time for the intended opening date. The building of Rivendell was completed in record time, on budget, and in a spirit of love, joy, and harmony whose existence is another part of the mystery which pervades its beginnings. The very first retreat group arrived on June 1st; June 2nd welcomed more than 100 guests to the opening and dedication, and on June 9th nearly 200 people made their way to Rivendell for the two hour open house. Rivendell retreat was underway only twenty-one months after Howard and Shirley's lunch with Ken and Ruth. It was now moving into a new stage of the journey with a great awareness of the mystery and the miraculous that had brought about the completion of the first adventure.

Come all you who are thirsty
Come to the waters
You who have no money,
come buy and eat
Come buy wine and milk
Without money and without cost

Isaiah 55:1

III.

Enfleshing and Sustaining the Vision

Envisioning the Hosting Community: Conflicting Models

I believe that Rivendell's core community, like its physical existence, came about because of a vision that was held and passed on by a few people. When construction had begun and the Rivendell building was underway, Shirley and Kathi created a steering committee that would be responsible for shaping Rivendell's inner life. When they called the steering committee together to discuss the vision for the retreat hosting community for the first time, they started the meeting with this insight: "The presence of people is going to make Rivendell a place of prayer and simplicity. The building creates a lot, but a group of people who are there will enflesh this."

The steering committee defined Rivendell primarily as "a Christian *community* rooted in the practiced traditions of prayer, silence, simplicity, and hospitality"[1] which upholds as its vision

---

1. Thanks goes to Loren Balisky for crafting Rivendell's first vision statement: "Situated on BC's Bowen Island, Rivendell is a Christian community rooted in the practiced traditions of prayer, silence, simplicity, and hospitality; offering a place of welcome to individuals and small groups who are seeking spiritual renewal, respite, and growth, accessible to those of limited resources and special needs."

the four values of accessibility, availability, accountability, and ambiance[2]. Thus it became clear that a strong and sustainable core community that would support the life of Rivendell was central to the vision for the retreat center. With its role delineated, nomenclature and definitions became two driving concerns shaping the development of the hosting community.[3]

Eventually, after many clarifying discussions, they agreed that the hosting community would be called the "Core Community" and would shape Rivendell's life and vision by inviting retreatants to join the ongoing work and life of the retreat center during their time at Rivendell. With this understanding, the steering committee first attempted to outline the details of Rivendell's Core Community and find people who would enflesh this vision. It soon became apparent that there was a new vision arising for the Core Community.

Although some members of the steering committee thought a couple should be hired to live at Rivendell full time with volunteer community members for support (in my experience this is the way most retreat centers continue to operate), Kathi and other steering committee members had a different vision. Kathi had heard of a hosting model developed by Margaret and Marks McAvity at the Sorrento Retreat Center[4] based on intentional community building. She also wanted to integrate Nestucca's vision for accessibility and its practice of inviting retreatants to participate in the care of the retreat center as a spiritual practice during their retreat.[5]

2. Thanks goes to Marks McAvity for coining these four words after the community had been developing the underlying philosophies for several months and the need to articulate them in a memorable way for the hosts became evident while orienting groups to Rivendell.

3. Two key quotes from these early meetings are: "nomenclature is everything"-*Kathi Bentall* and "how we define community will shape all our decisions."-*Shirley Bentall*

4. Sorrento Retreat Center is a year-round Anglican retreat center in Sorrento, British Columbia.

5. Nestucca was a Catholic retreat center in Western Washington founded and run by Andy Dufner, SJ. It closed in 2012.

"A paid staff detracts from a retreatant's experience," Kathi argued. A hired staff, she suggested, tends to create an environment in which both retreatants and staff expect the paid hosts to do everything. While this could be considered a good thing, in a retreat context it can prevent retreatants from experiencing meaningful forms of participation in the retreat Community. Ultimately they had to decide: which of these two philosophies, paid staff or volunteer Core Community, would be most likely to create the community envisioned for Rivendell? This question consumed the steering committee as they tried to shape the hosting community. Rivendell's opening day was quickly approaching and the steering committee still had not decided what the Core Community should look like. They were only sure of one thing: that to create the spirit of community envisioned for Rivendell, the community members must have certain agreed-upon characteristics and a relationship with Jesus.

They decided to continue the discernment process by seeing who was interested in becoming a part of Rivendell's first hosting community. To find these people, the steering committee held a Day of Discernment. Everybody on the steering committee was asked to invite people they thought would be good to participate in the Rivendell Community. Several promising couples from Regent College were invited to represent the vision of paid hosts, and Kathi invited Margaret and Marks McAvity to represent the vision of a volunteer Core Community.

Kathi had met Margaret and Marks McAvity while she was leading a retreat at Sorrento[6], where Marks was director, and they had connected immediately. When Margaret and Marks finished working at Sorrento they moved to Vancouver, British Columbia for Margaret to pursue a Masters of Divinity at the Vancouver School of Theology. While in Vancouver Marks reconnected with an old friend from Sorrento who had ties to Rivendell and Margaret reconnected with Kathi when she fulfilled her VST field placement requirement at the Listening Post.

Many ideas and visions were transformed into workable plans as these two women shared their experiences, their hopes,

6. "Sorrento" refers to the Sorrento Retreat Center.

and their wisdom with one another during Rivendell's formative years. Margaret and Marks had learned valuable lessons from their experience directing the Sorrento retreat center with a volunteer hosting community. They had learned about boundaries and burnout and they had learned that you need a consistent community of people volunteering from a position of strength in order to have a vital, sustainable retreat center. Now Margaret was sharing these experiences and many others with Kathi, making valuable contributions to Rivendell's community formation behind the scenes long before they became the hub of its core community.

As Kathi spoke with Margaret, she knew that if anyone would be able to give the philosophy of a volunteer community the best chance, it was Margaret and Marks. But when Kathi had invited them to come to the first discernment day and consider becoming part of the Rivendell community they declined. "We are still tired from our past retreat work," they said, "Margaret is about to graduate, and we just need some time for rest and personal discernment—not a new commitment!" But although neither Margaret nor Marks were at the discernment meetings, their presence was not unfelt. For as Kathi prepared the activities for the community discernment meeting, she was hearing about Margaret's experiences with the discernment process and activities used for the Sorrento retreat community and these ideas were shaping that day's activities.

The night before the meeting, Kathi had a dream. In the dream, her daughter Tasha was caring for the children during the discernment meeting. At the end of the meeting there was a tie in the vote over who should be chosen for the leadership, Kathi or a young couple. Kathi awoke from her dream to a phone call: the babysitter booked for the day was canceling. Kathi knew that Tasha was available so she called her to see if she could fill in. After reflecting on her dream and writing it in her journal, Kathi prepared herself: The day of the discernment meeting arrived.

Kathi had designed a series of activities for the day to give people an idea of what retreat work would be like. As the final activity in the day, Kathi used a rug on the floor to represent three concentric circles. The more commitment each person felt to the Rivendell community, the closer to the center they were to stand. One woman stood in the very center, representing a young family, but she and her family did not ultimately commit to Rivendell. Others were scattered over the rug in various relations to the center. John and Wendy Hardy, who became part of the first Core Community, were standing on the extreme edge of the carpet. They lifted their toes. Kathi and Caryn Stelk, who also became part of Rivendell's first Core Community, each took one foot off the carpet while keeping one foot just on its edge.

At the end of the day, the conclusion mirrored Kathi's dream: there was an equal representation for her (and the vision she represented) and the vision of hired community leaders. The steering committee decided to give the vision of a paid staff a three month trial and David and Shauna Anderson were offered a three month contract because, as Tasha said, "watching David with his child made her convinced that if they were going to pick someone, David was it." David and Shauna moved into Rivendell with their son Aiden a week before Rivendell opened. They worked hard, both within the building and without, preparing the place for retreatants.

Moving to a Sustainable Volunteer Hosting Community

The steering committee originally hired David and Shauna Anderson as full-time, live-in hosts for the Rivendell Lodge but it soon became evident that a paid staff was not financially sustainable. Rivendell's vision to make retreat space available and accessible to people regardless of financial means was being threatened. Costs had to remain low to sustain the vision and a full-time salary was a big expense. As the summer progressed, Rivendell's income could not sustain a salary and regular upkeep costs. So Kathi and her parents began considering who they might invite to be part of a volunteer core community. They both thought of Marilyn Gullison.

Marilyn was taking a diploma in spiritual formation from Carey College, in Vancouver, BC, at the time of life when many people retire. Like Margaret, Marilyn also had course requirements that drew her into a relationship with Kathi during Rivendell's community formation. One of the expectations of the spiritual formation program was that each student journey with a spiritual director. Marilyn had known Shirley Bentall for many years and thought she had heard that her daughter, Kathi, was a spiritual director so she called her and arranged to meet with her over coffee. Kathi met Marilyn, and afterwards, as she was driving away, she suddenly thought, "Marilyn should be part of it!" Kathi called her soon after they had met for coffee and told her that she and Howard and Shirley wanted to know if Marilyn would join Rivendell's first volunteer core community. Marilyn agreed, and thus became the very first officially invited Volunteer Core Community member, or "Watchkeeper."[7]She has continued to be part of the Rivendell community since its inception.

In late August, as the Anderson's contract was ending and the steering committee, realizing that the present situation was not financially sustainable, was beginning to try out the vision of a volunteer Core Community, Margaret and Marks' period of rest and discernment after Margaret's graduation was concluding. At this timely moment, Margaret and Marks called Kathi. They had reconsidered. They now felt rested, they said, and ready to give the volunteer model of community another try. Thus, in a little home in Caulfeild, British Columbia Shirley and Howard, Kathi, Marilyn, Margaret and Marks came together for the first time to embark on a six month trial that became an enduring success.

When Margaret and Marks agreed to come to Rivendell they stipulated that, while they wanted a volunteer Core Community, it was important that Rivendell reimburse all expenses related

7. This is another name, from Marks' Navy days, that is used sometimes to refer to each one who serves as a member of Rivendell's volunteer core community.

to Rivendell hosting responsibilities. They also required that the retreat center had to have a large enough and strong enough Core Community to allow everyone freedom to take vacations, visit family, help out in family emergencies, and have some time for "normal life." With this requirement in mind, they gathered those who had already been serving Rivendell, officially or not, as a volunteer core community. To John and Wendy Hardy's great surprise, they were invited to this gathering.

John and Wendy had worked with Paul Stevens, offering Spiritual Direction in one of his classes when Rivendell was being developed. Paul approached them saying that he and his wife, Gail, had been praying about the Rivendell community and thought John and Wendy would be perfect for it. They were very hesitant. At first they refused, but finally agreed to attend the day of discernment held by the steering committee. As previously described, when the meaning of the concentric circles was made clear, John and Wendy, already on the periphery, moved their feet off the rug completely. At this same meeting, John, unaware that he was speaking prophetically said, "What you need is retired people with lots of energy" (although he added, somewhat less prophetically, "more energy than we have!"). When this discernment meeting concluded, John and Wendy thought that their involvement with Rivendell was also over. David and Shauna Anderson, however, knew John and Wendy well, and during their three months at Rivendell, they asked them to fill in when they wanted to get off the island.

When Margaret and Marks began at Rivendell, John and Wendy again assumed that their involvement with Rivendell was over. Now, to their surprise, they were invited to a gathering of the Rivendell Volunteer Core Community and their belonging affirmed. Although they still considered themselves on the outside, the rest of the "Watchkeepers," warmly and unreservedly included them. They thus unwittingly became part of the original Core and continue as such. Within the year the hosts of Rivendell also included Caryn Stelk, Mary Leslie, Barbara and Gilli McLaren, Lorraine Lamarre, and Bev Rogers. On its Ten Year Anniversary, the Core Community had grown from the original ten to include many other volunteer hosts.

The time these women and men have regularly given to Rivendell for over ten years is an incredible gift given by those who have reached or passed the age of retirement—a gift that goes beyond financial compensation. While each year an honorarium is given to each of Rivendell's hosts as thanks, there is no salary that could compensate for the love and the blessings, the wisdom and the discernment, and the witness of the peace and joy of a life lived for others that they give for the wider Rivendell Retreat community. It is this seasoning of life that deepens the ambiance more than vision alone could do. Individually and as a community, the elders who comprise the Core Community embody Rivendell's vision, sacredly holding and tending it as a place of welcome and refreshment for all, regardless of background, beliefs, or socio-economic status, who thirst for spiritual renewal.

Practices for Personal Sustainability

While the people called to serve as hosts at Rivendell are known to be people able to serve from a position of strength, it is necessary to attend to the ongoing care and health of the members of the Core Community so they can continue to do so. The community has developed practices and rhythms that foster health and prevent burnout in their hosting community.

For one thing, while recognizing that hosting is the central service of the Core Community,[8] each person also has complete freedom to choose the amount of their service and is released from any pressure to do more than they are able. This is expressed

8. A line from the Rivendell Community covenant reads, "Although our amount of hosting service at Rivendell varies considerably, each of us recognizes that it is this service which ultimately binds us, and it is the one for which we are most accountable."

clearly in one line in the covenant: "We honor each other's varied commitments, knowing that others in the community are available to be present as hosts in our absence." The freedom to choose their own hosting times without pressure to host more than they are willing means that the hosts can serve when they have time and energy, not out of exhaustion, burnout, or coercion.

Not only are the hosts invited to serve when they are able, rather than on demand, they are also welcome to host in their own unique way. Some may invite retreatants back to Wisteria for dinner and conversation, others may not. Some prefer to work in the office while others prefer working around the lodge or grounds. Still others feel it is part of their calling at Rivendell to be intentional about providing opportunities for Spiritual Direction to retreatants.

Furthermore, each host is also given freedom to lead the 5pm worship time in their own style. There are as many ways to host at Rivendell as there are hosts. These opportunities for self-expression in their manner of hosting and leading at Rivendell mean that each member of the Core Community can serve from their strengths and be energized by their service. The diversity of service is also a great blessing to Rivendell because it allows for the unique giftedness of each host to be offered to the retreat community while they are hosting.

Since the hosts take turns watchkeeping, rather than hosting together, community building activities are important, reminding them of their common purpose. Each year the Core Community members join together three times for retreats intended to nourish and refresh them both personally and spiritually. These retreats also build community and cover topics relevant to their watch keeping duties. Two maintenance weeks a year and other events that may be organized throughout also provide a chance for the Community to come together for refreshment and community with a common purpose. These practices of voluntary service, freedom to lead from personal giftedness, and rhythms of gathering regularly for community building, seem to prevent burnout and empower the Core Community to continue to lead with joy and energy.

Concentric Circles: Sustainability through Broader Community

As the visioning committee recognized, Rivendell's character would be primarily shaped, not by its buildings, but by its people. While this was applied initially to the hosting community, it has proven to include the wider community of Rivendell as well. The broader, multifaceted community also shapes Rivendell's unique character.

You may remember the rug with the concentric circle design that Kathi used on the day of discernment to give people a chance to show where they saw themselves in relation to the Rivendell community. Although this circle did not accurately reflect the state of how things turned out, except perhaps in opposites, it was an excellent picture of what Rivendell community life has become: an ever widening sphere of interconnected circles that begin at the center and flow outward into increasingly larger circles that together form the community which is Rivendell Retreat Center.

For more than ten years this retreat center has been shepherded by a thriving volunteer community of elders which dwells at the Core, or within the inner circle, of the much broader sphere which is the retreat community. These shepherds hold the vision of Rivendell as they listen, pray and bless all those who come to Rivendell. Although the hosts keep very busy with the daily needs of the building there is so much manual work needed to keep it running there is no way they can do it all while remaining available to the spiritual needs of those they welcome.

Enter, those who make up the next circle widening out from the center, the many day laborers, unpaid and sometimes paid, who give their time, energy, and expertise to take care of the building and the Core community. The number of unseen tasks taken care of by the people in this next concentric circle is endless and each one is necessary for the life of Rivendell. By coming over to scrub carpet spots, clean walls, or give a room a well-deserved deep cleaning; by catering the retreats of the core community, coming as a guest to lead one of these retreats, or by serving on the society board or foundation; by tending and creating new paths and gardens or caring for the Labyrinth; by felling dead trees and cutting them into rounds or by chopping these large rounds into useful firewood, these people form a circle of care for Rivendell that contributes to its well cared for look and prevents burnout in the Core community.

Many who consider themselves in the second concentric circle will also recognize themselves among those in the third and widest circle of the three: the Retreatants. By far, the largest and most inclusive circle is inhabited by those who come to Rivendell as retreatants. What defines a retreatant in the picture of the concentric circles is that they come primarily to receive the gift of retreat space that Rivendell offers and to tend their own inner spiritual life. All who come contribute to the spiritual life of Rivendell by their presence and to the physical life of Rivendell by making their own bed when they arrive and leaving their room and all other spaces they use during their retreat clean and ready to welcome the next person who will use it.

The image of the rug on discernment day is a good place to begin envisioning the interlacing communities that are Rivendell, but it is not complete so long as it remains static in our imaginations. The beauty of the image of the concentric circles is that it is not stagnant. Movement within the circle flows past hazy lines that distinguish each concentric circle from the others. While the Core Community is a strong presence felt at Rivendell's center, the hosts become retreatants three times a year during their Community retreats. Those in the second circles who contribute to the ongoing care of the building and grounds often recognize the need they come back to fill while on their own retreat at Rivendell. Finally, the retreatants in the widest ring, who come away for themselves often find meaning in the Benedictine practice of work as a way of tending their own spiritual journey during their stay, and in so doing contribute to the care of the building, the grounds, and the ongoing life of Rivendell. The community of Rivendell is more than a rug patterned with concentric circles, it is living art.

Folding the Sheets: A Benedictine Spirituality of Work

When my family and I moved to Bowen Island we wanted to serve Rivendell in whatever way would be most helpful, thus offering to become volunteers in the second concentric circle of the wider Rivendell community. We soon realized that this might take the shape of folding sheets. With a regularly high occupancy and 18 rooms, many of which have two single beds, there is a nearly constant need to wash bed and bath linens. So we offered our service and have occasionally had the opportunity to help with Rivendell laundry.

When we arrived for our first day of laundry duty we realized that we were getting in for more than we had bargained for. Separating the various linens into different piles, loading the washer and switching washed loads to the dryer was pretty simple and we soon got the hang of it. When we got to the folding, however, we realized that we were out of our league! I have been folding laundry with my mother since I was a child. I have taught my children how to hold their ends of the sheets and help me fold our sheets at home. When I came to Rivendell, however, I realized that none of us really knew how to fold sheets "the right way." We more or less just "slapped them together" so to speak. If our sheets looked like some semblance of a rectangle or square then it was considered a job well done. When we came to Rivendell our first lesson was "how to fold the laundry."

Folding the sheets at Rivendell is not just a job, it is a ritual: of love, of worship. It also has certain expectations of quality. So that the sheets look uniform when placed at the foot of each bed it is important that all sheets be folded the same way in spite of the diversity of people who fold them. Learning this way has become a sort of comedic "rite of initiation." So please, let me initiate you.

First you take the top and bottom corners and fold them together lengthwise. Now pull the sheet tight to make sure that the entire length of the sheet lines up properly; never underestimate the importance of a good strong tug to make the sheet behave. Each sheet has to be pulled tightly before and after each fold to compensate for not ironing each one. Fold the sheet lengthwise twice. Every corner needs to meet exactly when making each fold and edges that hang sloppily out are not permitted.

When the sheet looks like a long, narrow rectangle, then the folders move toward each other (after one more pull to make sure the edges are good and tight). Now make the long narrow line into a tight square cube of sheet about 1 square foot by folding the length in thirds. This technique is sometimes attributed to Margaret McAvity, although this rhythm of sheet folding was not developed by her alone, but in concert with many others over the years. Furthermore, towels, bathmats, pillow cases and other linens are also folded with intention. Although it may initially sound funny to many of us, who may not care how our laundry is folded, so long as it eventually makes it into the drawers, folding the sheets is considered a spiritual practice. Furthermore, the practice of prayer is woven into the practice of carrying out the many unnoticed yet necessary daily tasks with intention. Most laundry items, for example, are folded into thirds at some point in the folding process thereby making an intentional opportunity to prayerfully fold, "in the name of the Father, the Son, and the Holy Spirit."

Folding the sheets as a spiritual practice has become for me a symbol representing the way the Hosts view work here at Rivendell. Like the dessert Abbas and Ammas who maintained that the straw of daily work could become the gold of unceasing prayer, the hosts of Rivendell carry out the repetitive and menial tasks of Rivendell's upkeep as an act of prayer and they invite retreatants and volunteers to do likewise. Carrying out daily repetitive jobs in a prayerful way has had a strong influence on the ambiance at Rivendell. While it may be tempting to rush through one job with an eye on the endless list of all the jobs still to do, keeping focused on the way in which the job is done understands that a job done peacefully, creates a more peaceful ambiance. When Howard

Bentall was living at Rivendell as the first Elder in Residence[9], he used to sit in his chair and watch the hosts go by as they were doing their various jobs. If they would rush by he would call out as a gentle and teasing reminder, "there is a speed limit around here." He was helping them remember their principle that the way the work is done at Rivendell is important.

There are many daily tasks at Rivendell that, while they may seem to go unappreciated or unnoticed, cultivate the ambiance of peace, mindfulness and prayer that pervades Rivendell. Changing lightbulbs, setting up the rooms for new retreatants arriving, answering emails, arranging the bookings, regular maintenance, chopping wood, gardening, re-supplying regular needs, re-organizing the drawers and cupboards that Shirley abundantly provided, tending the compost, maintaining the trails, and a myriad of other tasks upon which retreatants unknowingly depend. This is the work that is done quietly behind the scenes. It is a gift of service and an activity of prayer that people may not see.

9. Shirley Bentall died in March, 2005. Shortly after that her husband, Howard Bentall, came to live in Willow, a housekeeping room on the lower level of the lodge, for the last 2 1/2 years of his life. He became the first elder in residence and the only person who ever lived at Rivendell.

When my family and I were taught how to set up rooms, for example, the last item on the list is "say a prayer for the next retreatant who will be using this room during their retreat." This made me realize that all these years, every time one of the Watch keepers sets up a room for the next retreatant, they are holding that retreatant in prayer. I realized through my own experience at Rivendell that it is not only that all these "care taking" jobs are done, it is that they are done as a spiritual act. The way in which they are done shapes the heart of Rivendell as much as the warm welcome that retreatants experience on their arrival, or the spiritual direction that they may receive during their stay. It is the cultivation of a spirit of ceaseless prayer and humility that is the true work of these tasks, and is the true work that the Rivendell community remembers and holds, giving meaning to even the most "meaningless" tasks.

IV.

Living Out the Vision

Rivendell's physical existence was birthed from a vision that was held and shared by a few people. Rivendell's community also had its roots in vision, a rare vision of a volunteer community of elders who would invite retreatants and other volunteers to participate in the life and care of Rivendell. The sustained life and ongoing development of Rivendell over the years has continued in this tradition, being guided by vision. The original principles continue to be the four pillars of its current vision: accessibility, availability, attention to ambiance, and accountability. Several of the key developments over the years illustrate the way this vision has been worked out in Rivendell's maturation.

The first of these principles, accessibility, has perhaps been the most important principle guiding Rivendell's development. It was the main motivation behind trying a volunteer core community and is the reason why, when asked how much a night at Rivendell costs, retreatants are simply encouraged to, "pay generously within what you can afford" with tax receipts given for payments over $60 per night per retreatant.[1] In this, as in everything else, the hosts hold the vision and invite retreatants to participate in the Rivendell community by contributing as they are able to this principle of accessibility, not just for the tax receipt but so that

1. The minimum payment required to receive a tax receipt is subject to annual change for inflation. It is also important to keep in mind that this low cost per nightly stay reflects the impact of a volunteer Core Community in place of a paid staff.

those who are able to come to Rivendell because of this principle can continue to do so. All who come to Rivendell are invited to participate in a microcosm of a vision of a world characterized by the social equality envisioned by Isaiah: "You who have no money, come buy wine and milk without money and without cost.[2]"

The principle of accessibility, with its sister principle, availability, also motivated the special mandate and ministry of The Rivendell Cottage, the discussion around the inclusion of children, and the creation of the Labyrinth.

The Cottage: It's Special Mandate and Ministry

Once, when Shirley was driving, she drove past a mother with her children standing at a bus stop. It was a very cold, rainy day and Shirley thought of their discomfort. She stopped her car, turned around and picked them up, giving them a ride to their destination. She and the woman developed a friendship from this encounter that they maintained over many years. When the cottage at Rivendell was being conceived of and built, Shirley recalled her experience with this woman and her family as her inspiration for this cottage. Families, refugees, and those unexpectedly in need of a safe place for retreat after an emergency, were some of the people Shirley had in mind when she envisioned the Rivendell cottage. In keeping with this vision, the cottage was built on the far side of the driveway, away from the main lodge. The physical distance between the two buildings provides privacy and a natural sound barrier between the lodge and the cottage which is probably appreciated both by the children staying at the cottage and the retreatants in the lodge.

The hosts at Rivendell continue to protect the original vision for the Cottage and hold in their hearts and memories many touching stories about families who have stayed there. One such story was found among Shirley's keepsakes. A young family came from Vancouver's Downtown Eastside to use the cottage during Rivendell's first year. After that visit the mother sent the following thank-you letter to Shirley. It explained the importance of having

2. Isaiah 55:1 NIV.

a place like the cottage available for her family. This letter was obviously special to Shirley because many years after her death, it was found in her file containing only a few special cards and notes about Rivendell.

> Dear Shirley,
>
> I am on my way back home to the Downtown Eastside with my family—my husband and our five daughters. We rarely have the chance to leave our neighborhood and enjoy the beauty of nature, the silence, the space. We have lived in the Downtown Eastside in a Christian community for ten years, but have had a difficult time finding retreat places that will welcome our children also. After all, they really need to connect with other realities than their day to day lives. My girls had a wonderful time. It was especially relaxing for us as the areas surrounding this home are very safe for conscientious kids. This little home is very warm and plenty spacious for even our big family. Thank you for providing the place that accommodated a very special family get away. P.S. Marks and Margaret were terrific hosts and have a lovely way with little ones.

Baby Steps: Welcoming the Children

The mandate of the cottage implicitly makes retreat accessible to children but figuring out how to welcome children while also honoring the attention to ambiance principle has been a challenge over the years. While some retreat centers hold "Family Retreat" weeks[3] Rivendell offers an unstructured space and encourages minimal programming to leave time for personal reflection and stillness. When you walk in, it is (usually) quiet and people may be seen walking slowly, closing doors quietly, reading, journalling, or sitting in silence gazing out one of the many large windows; sometimes you will see (or hear) two or more adults engaged in deep, adult conversation. Thus Rivendell seems primarily for adults. And yet children have a place, if somewhat uncertain, in Rivendell's history and life.

Throughout ten years of Rivendell community meeting minutes the discussion about children continues to surface but without resolution. At one time, it is recorded, someone asked at a meeting if they should make a rule against allowing children at Rivendell, but no answer was forthcoming at that meeting, nor at any of the following ones for which I had minutes.

There are some real concerns about welcoming children. First, one of Rivendell's mandates is to preserve an ambiance for retreatants that is conducive to inner reflection and therefore values quiet. Children can be busy, noisy, unpredictable, and very distracting and constantly "shushing" them is unlikely to foster a love of retreat. Another concern is that a child will take away from a parent's much needed personal retreat. If both parents come and bring a toddler in tow, than one parent may spend the retreat running distractedly around after the child while the other parent enjoys his (or her) retreat. Taking turns to go away for individual retreats often facilitates a better experience for everyone. A weekend retreat is a gift of love that one spouse can give to the other. There are times, however, when an entire family is in need of some

---

3. cf Naramata Center for an example of family retreat programming.

retreat time together to reconnect and find renewal and for this there is the cottage with its unique mandate and placement.

Children have also been involved at the lodge in life-giving ways. Since many of the members of the Core Community are actively involved grandparents, many have occasionally brought their grandchildren with them when they host. Barbara and Gilli's granddaughter, Devyani, has been familiar with Rivendell since she was five years old. She learned the "ritual" of folding the sheets and loves helping her grandparents fold laundry when she gets the special opportunity to stay with them for a night or two of their watch. "Once in a while," Barbara told me, with a bit of a chuckle, "our granddaughter would be talking to someone outside of Rivendell and proudly refer to herself as part of the Rivendell Community."

Marilyn's grandson Cameron has also joined his grandmother at Rivendell. Marilyn has always been very conscientious about the ambiance of Rivendell and aware of how children, even her own grandson, can threaten this ambiance. Thus she has brought her grandson with her infrequently. When she brought her little grandson, she always told him that the five o'clock worship time was for adults. Once, however, while Cameron was there, another young child staying at Rivendell came to the worship time with his parents. When Marilyn saw this, she went and told Cameron that he too could join them that day. As a result of this experience, Marilyn, while still protective over the retreat environment, reflects that, "When you can incorporate the children, it can make a beautiful worship experience."

Kathi has also found ways to welcome children at Rivendell and introduce them to retreat. She has held a small weekend retreat for young mothers with nursing babies. The mothers and babies stayed at the cottage during the retreat. It was an experiment. Kathi knew all the mothers and babies and that their parenting style was conducive to retreat, but still she was taking a risk in her willingness to welcome young mothers, who, while usually in great need of retreat, find it elusive. This retreat went well and the mothers were refreshed and renewed at the end of the weekend. Kathi also brought her granddaughter, Maya, to the Rivendell cottage for Maya's first retreat on her sixth birthday and they have kept this tradition each year since.

I too have brought each of my daughters to Rivendell for a "mother-daughter" retreat weekend. Both of these retreats were wonderful. I took my oldest daughter Melissa on her first retreat when she was ten years old. I had gone on several of my own retreats and she wanted me to show her what I did while I was away. When we arrived, Margaret and Marks, who were hosting that weekend, were warm and friendly and made us feel truly welcome.

We spent the weekend curled up in front of a fire in Quince, a little sitting room just down the hall from our bedroom on the third floor. We read, talked quietly and reflectively together, and sometimes we just sat together in silence before the hypnotizing fire. At the end of this retreat, Melissa asked if we could call home and stay a few more days. When this was not an option she asked if we could do this every fourth week by alternating biweekly retreats: one by myself, one with her, ad infinitum. I too cherished this time we shared together.

My youngest daughter, Alexis, was only eight when I took her for her first retreat and I was concerned about us being a distraction for retreatants. She had no interest in going on a retreat until her sister returned from her's with a glowing report and frequent requests for another. Soon after her older sister's retreat, Alexis asked me to take her. Thankfully Kathi booked us into the cottage to give space for Alexis's energy and her love of freedom and physical activity. When we arrived Alexis and I were given the same warm welcome that had been extended to her older sister.

Wildlife and the labyrinth defined my retreat with Alexis. Alexis found silence and reflection effortless as she let nature teach her about retreat. Once she stopped, and watched a squirrel so patiently that we saw it, after looking cautiously around, whisk down into some unseen area and bring forth a nut from its secret stash.

Alexis also walked the labyrinth so often, with feet shod or bare, that she came to know many of the stones by the feel of their contours and texture. She still remembers, years later that, "there was one very soft black rock" she particularly liked. Alexis and I did not sit by the fire very often that weekend, instead we were being re-created and renewed by nature.

The lodge has also hosted a few groups offering retreats geared to children. Two parent-child retreats have been offered in Rivendell's past and one retreat for older children (12+). At the first parent-child retreat, Howard Bentall[4], his strong spirit shining through his frail, aging body, exuberantly acted out the children's very physical prayer of thanks (which included a jump) before dinner one evening. His obvious delight in the children was a gift to everyone around him.

It is true that children are a wild card, even more at Rivendell than in everyday life, because of the deep silence and peace that pervades the place and the desire to keep the ambiance protected for *all* retreatants. Thankfully, however, since its inception, Rivendell has tried in various ways and at various times, to open its arms to the little children as well as the big ones, while also trying to protect and guard Rivendell as a haven of silence and solace for all who come through its doors.

The Labyrinth

The Labyrinth is situated on public land at the base of the hill on which perches the Lodge and is open to Bowen Island's general public. When the vision of building a Labyrinth was beginning to rise among the Rivendell community, Kathi bumped into Maggie Cummings and shared the idea with her. Maggie was a long time resident of Bowen Island who was also on the Parks and Trails committee. Maggie loved the idea and both thought it could be built on public land on Cates Hill and available to everyone. Kathi knew a good idea when she had one and brought it back to the rest of the Rivendell Community to see what they thought.

Maggie's suggestion beautifully dovetailed with Rivendell's principle of accessibility. The Labyrinth would not be limited

---

4. Elder in Residence at the time.

to use by retreatants alone but would be accessible to their near neighbors on Cates Hill and to any others who wanted to make the pilgrimage. With great excitement they began the land use application process and Bruce Haggerstone came on board to design the Labyrinth.

The Labyrinth at Rivendell is made in the design of the Labyrinth at Chartres and was meticulously planned. After Bruce had figured out how to make the Labyrinth he used rope to outline the path for the rocks. Without his meticulous attention to detail and planning, such a complicated Labyrinth would never have made it off the ground. In addition to the focused work of Bruce, it also took a huge amount of volunteer labor to realize the outline on the ground. Volunteers devoted hours to finding each of the huge rocks that make up the Labyrinth. Its rocks, like icebergs, are much bigger than they look from the surface, with roots that go deep into the ground beneath each small step you take when walking the labyrinth. The Labyrinth was blessed on Rivendell's fifth anniversary in 2007.

The Labyrinth is the project in Rivendell history that still brings that look of alarm into the eyes of those who were involved when you ask them about it. Try it sometime. Just casually mention, "have you ever thought about building another Labyrinth?" and you'll see what I mean. The building of the Labyrinth is the feat about which is said, "we are very glad we did it, but it was too much work to ever do again." So why then, would they think it worth the work? What is it about a Labyrinth that is so special? While it is great to have a beautiful interactive landscape to offer the neighbors and further the accessibility principle but accessibility only confirmed the location, it did not spark the initial vision for this communal work of sacred art.

The Labyrinth was worth it for many reasons, not least because it uniquely shapes the life and practice of prayer: it models for us new ways of going deeper by drawing on ancient practices to renew and expand our present forms of prayer; it offers a form of embodied prayer, reminding us that we can pray as whole people, not just disembodied spirits; and it makes an inviting practice of prayer accessible to the wider island community.

The Labyrinth, the children, and the cottage challenge us, in the living vision of the Rivendell Retreat Center, to extend our practice of contemplation to those who are on the margins of our lives and welcome the outcast, the children, and the neighbor as Jesus did.

V.

Renewing the Vision

Rivendell's development was rooted in vision, but it is not enough to simply begin with vision and keep it going without. Eventually things change enough that the original vision has to either be renewed or stagnate. After ten years, it seemed that Rivendell's had reached this point and in response, the Center's tenth year saw, not only her Anniversary celebration but a renewal of vision. The development of new spiritual rhythms, formation of the Succession Committee, honoring Rivendell's Elders in Residence, recognizing and strengthening the concentric circles of the wider Rivendell community, building the new Sanctuary, and beginning development on the Second Site, were the most significant signs of the renewal.

New Spiritual Rhythms

First, the Core Community added a new spiritual rhythm: 8am centering prayer. For ten years the daily 5pm gathering for worship was the only structured rhythm at Rivendell. The early emphasis on minimal programming hindered all considerations about adding more structure to the day. After much contemplation, however, the Core Community felt that it would be retaining the original vision and attending well to the ambiance to add an early morning silent prayer time to the daily rhythm. This early morning gathering for silence has proven to be a wonderful addition to the rhythms of

Rivendell, wrapping the day from beginning to end in prayer for the hosts and the retreatants who join them.

The Hosting Community also, after keeping programming off their job descriptions for a decade, piloted two new retreats organized and offered by themselves, one at Advent and one at Easter. These retreats have been well received but the Core Community continues to evaluate this new programming in light of Rivendell's vision and principles.

Replacing Ourselves: Forming a Succession Committee

In the same year the Core Community created a new committee: the Succession Committee. Recognizing that the trend and challenges of aging are only going to continue, the hosting community realized that in order to keep a healthy Core they need to welcome new and younger elders. The Succession Committee formalized the discernment process by which elders can explore becoming part of the Core Community. It continues to actively seek spiritually mature elders, inviting them to join the discernment process and consider service as hosts to the wider Rivendell Community.

Affirming the Gifts of Eldership: Elders in Residence

The renewal of vision in Rivendell's tenth year also sparked a new desire to affirm the gifts of eldership. During a retreat for Core Community members that focused on the importance of eldership, the Core Community formally named a "core within the Core" by affirming those hosts who had aged beyond the energy required for much regular hosting. These community members were now invited to continue sharing their presence with the Rivendell community as Elders in Residence. Howard Bentall was formally recognized as Rivendell's first Elder in Residence in honor of the two and a half years he lived in residence in Willow. Lorraine Lamarre SSA, though not living as a full time resident at Rivendell, was named an official Elder in Residence at that retreat in 2012. Lorraine was honored for her years of commitment to Rivendell and the value of her ongoing contribution affirmed[1].

Naming and Strengthening Concentric Circles of Community

The fresh vision for Rivendell encompassed new rhythms for retreatants, new practices to nurture the Core Community, and a new appreciation of the importance of those in the second concentric circle of Rivendell's wider community. At the business level this looked like clarifying and affirming the roles of the Rivendell Foundation and the Rivendell Society (the Board)[2]. The main focus was on strengthening the board so that it could actively support the life of Rivendell. Kathi recognized that an empowered Board could help uphold the retreat center's vision and principles by articulating, in those areas where it would strengthen the Rivendell community, more detailed policies and procedures.

At the community level, the hosting community affirmed among themselves the continued importance of the many people who, although not part of the Core Community, are willing to be involved in the daily needs, the cleaning, and the maintenance of the Rivendell buildings and grounds. In conclusion, the burst of energy that came with the renewed vision seems to have strengthened the webs of appreciation for the many different types of community that work together to make Rivendell a vibrant retreat community.

1. Sr. Lorraine Lamarre died on November 26, 2013.

2. The Rivendell Foundation and the Rivendell were the legal bodies created to build and operate Rivendell. The Rivendell Foundation is the legal Charitable funding organization and the Rivendell Society is the legal Charitable operating society, otherwise known as the board.

Coming Full Circle: Completing the Original Vision

With all the newness that characterized the beginning of Rivendell's next decade, ironically the two biggest "new things" hearkened back to the old. In the tenth year, at the exact same time, more by mystery than plan, the design and construction of the stand alone Sanctuary and the beginning of the development of the Second Site happened, both of which had been envisioned but not realized by Rivendell's first steering committee.

The New Sanctuary

The new sanctuary was designed by Don Nicholson, who you may remember, was also the architect for the first Rivendell buildings to adorn the top of Cates' Hill. The sanctuary is nestled in the crook of the hill among tall trees. It sits at the end of the parking lot, just below the Cottage, just above the Lodge. The path that wanders from the cottage and past the Sanctuary leads down to the Labyrinth. In keeping with the principles of accessibility and availability, it remains open at all times and to all who wish to visit it. Since its completion, neighbors and retreatants alike find their way up the hill to enjoy the peace and stillness they find there.

When Kathi, Tim Scorer, chair of the Rivendell Board, Margaret, Marks, and Don Nicholson met to talk about the sanctuary they did not consult the original vision, yet the similarities between the original vision and the present one are amazing. At the dedication, Rita Kranabetter, who had been on Rivendell's first steering committee, brought her journal and read out to us what she had recorded from one of their meetings around their vision for a chapel. This was their original vision: "outside with walkway, round, floor heated, a sacred space to be used only for prayer, enough room to draw the community together, benches along the wall, and cushions, non-intrusive for retreatants or for others in the community."[3] Rather than build the chapel right away, the orig-

---

3. an excerpt from Rita Kranabetter's unpublished personal notes taken at a steering committee meeting.

inal steering committee decided to use the room that Shirley has designed to be the library as the prayer room until the envisioned chapel was built. The library was moved to Hawthorne[4] and it was ten years before the sanctuary came into existence.

As those gathered heard Rita's words, there were exclamations of wonder and surprise. Looking around at the entire community and the Board gathered comfortably in the new chapel, sitting on the benches along the wall, leaning against or ensconced on cushions in the nautilus shaped chapel, feeling the heat of the floor with their feet, recalling the slow walk from the lodge, across the parking lot and along the short, gently curving walkway sheltered by encircling trees, to the door where they had removed their shoes, it was impossible to miss the similarities between the original vision that had been hidden in the center of Rita's rough-lined spiral ring notebook for a decade and the realized vision of the present day without feeling awe.

As those who gathered to dedicate the long awaited sanctuary sat emsbraced by mystery and unity with the past, and as each shared their blessings for the new sanctuary, feelings of homecoming and completion filled the place. It seemed as though the original vision had been waiting for this time, these people, and

4. Hawthorne is a sitting room for retreatants use on the second floor.

this place, for fulfillment. A ten year gestation period of hope and patience, culminating in the final realization of the sanctuary, a separate structure dedicated wholly to prayer and worship, and the final stage of development for the Lodge site.

The Second Site: Developing the Rivendell Hermitage

In Rivendell's tenth year, after waiting through setbacks, complications, and disappointments, the development of Rivendell's Second Site also began. Originally Kathi and her mother shared a vision of a Retreat Center in two locations. One site was envisioned primarily for groups and the other for individuals, with an emphasis on silence and solitude. Recall in the first chapter, Shirley's agenda for the development of Rivendell was organized like this: *First Phase*: 1. Prepare sketches and plans for the first site, with cost estimates and time frame; 2. Figure out all the financial, legal, and organizational aspects necessary to ensure the completion of the current development and its ongoing sustainability; 3. Select an appropriate second site. *Second Phase*: Cates Hill. *Third Phase*: Second Site. While Rivendell was being built, Wolfgang took Shirley and Kathi to another site, one in Cowan Point on the south end of Bowen Island that he thought would work well for the Second Site. But while the Lodge on Cates Hill was realized as the Second Phase of Rivendell's development, the Cowan Point property never really got off the ground. Two cabins were renovated and furnished and used occasionally by individual retreatants who had connections to the place or people, Kathi gathered a small visioning committee who spent some time planning Rivendell's third phase, but it remained relatively embryonic until Rivendell's tenth year.[5]

---

5. One year before its tenth anniversary, I became part of the Rivendell story, in particular with the Hermitage development. As I write this section about the development of the Hermitage I intend to emulate the writer of Acts. When Luke begins to accompany Paul on his journeys his perspective and voice naturally shift from the third person to a first person account. I too, as I join the Rivendell community at this stage of its developmental journey, imitate Luke's device by joining my voice with the voices of its founders.

One: As we come together to prepare the shelters for those who come here looking for rest, respite, and connection with the Holy One, we pray for them, that they may feel the embrace of your love as they are embraced by these shelters and this place, a living sanctuary.

All: May the work of our hands and the meditation of our hearts be pleasing to you, O Lord.

Jennifer Kerr Graves

from *Readings and Prayers for the Building of the Hermitages*

VI.

The Hermitage: Holding the Vision

A Unique Site and Focus

As we begin the story of the Hermitage development, I would like to take some time to clarify the uniqueness of each site connected with the Rivendell Retreat Center. The Lodge is fully introduced by the earlier part of this story and leaves only the introduction of the Hermitage to this latter part of the tale.

There are two types of buildings at the Hermitage: a main house and five little sleeping shelters, or cabins. Working closely with Don Nicholson, architect for the Rivendell Lodge, and Barbara Wahler, interior designer for both the Sanctuary and the Hermitage main house, we designed each of the Hermitage spaces with great intentionality.

I began my writing for this section in the 107 square foot shelter and will spend most of my time there. It is inviting and cozy. It has a little wood stove with a small pot in which to boil a cup of tea; a comfortable chair; an extra long twin bed with shelves at the head and foot; a unique wooden table; a stool; an all-important lug-a-loo for nights; some hooks on the wall, and a small dresser for my clothes. The interior is rough walls painted a warm white and unadorned except for a small mirror. The exterior is sided with untreated cedar siding and has a tar and paper roof that slopes back from the sliding patio door entrance.

Whenever my computer battery ran low and I was getting hungry I moved from the little shelter in which I was writing to the main house because it has a kitchen, plumbing, and electricity. One day, thanks to the generosity of a woman from the visioning committee, there was some food in the fridge she labeled, "prepared with love for those who work here, enjoy." Normally I would have to bring my own food with me, preparing it and cleaning up afterwards. I chose two stuffed vegetables that day and put them in the top of the double oven that is in the kitchen. I plugged my computer into the wall outlet and sat at a personalized counter workspace on a comfortable wooden bar chair. In a place dedicated to solitude, sharing of the kitchen is minimized with individualized counter spaces, a well divided fridge, and a stove with a double oven design.

The main house was designed with the unique Hermitage principles in mind. The cream counters and warm red cupboards are calm and inviting, as are the cream walls, oak floors and all natural wood trim throughout the house. Four chairs are arranged around the central wood burning fireplace and at its end two more rotating chairs sit between it and a large window overlooking cedar, alder, hemlock, and fir trees, with a glimpse past them of the ocean. Two one-on-one rooms are also on this main floor where people can offer or receive spiritual direction. The prayer loft is the only room on the top level and looks over the main floor space. The lower level contains a large bathroom, laundry room, and two bedrooms for a host and retreatants who need greater accessibility than the wooded trails to the cabins permit. The lower level is primarily designed, however, as a multi-use art space, recognizing art as a meaningful form of spiritual engagement and expression. Nature also draws us closer to God, and large, abundant windows, four window seats, individual patios, and skylights bring the outdoor and the indoor close together, blending them in sight and sense throughout the building.

The land itself is quite isolated and an eleven kilometer pilgrimage from the ferry is required to get here. Hosts and retreatants alike are in silence while here and everyone brings their own bedding and food. The Hermitage retains the same mission statement and principles as the Rivendell Lodge. In addition it has a unique focus which is expressed through six additional principles, which are:

- *Solitude*—social spaciousness which allows for freedom to enter into silence;

- *Silence*—a protected space that encourages attentive listening to God and self;

- *Soul Hospitality*—Welcoming all who seek renewal and healing to a safe and inclusive Christian environment trusting in the generous love of the Creator;

- *Spaciousness*—a physical, spiritual and natural spaciousness that provides a non-intrusive, non-directive environment for freedom of spiritual expression and creativity. A space that honors life's rhythms and tensions;

- *Simplicity*—radical simplicity that respects the land by treating it gently and minimizing our footprint. A simplicity that is humanly and economically sustainable;

- *Sanctuary*—Nurturing nature's invisible embrace and beauty, recognizing and providing the opportunity to receive from a living sanctuary.

Holding the Vision

The story of the Hermitage development strikes me most as a story of both death and resurrection, long periods of gestation and the excitement of new life. I sit here writing at an old desk whose worn red paint reveals the aged wood, roughened and rounded beneath it. Through the clear, wood-framed rectangular window before me

I see the cedar and the hemlock which gently embrace my shelter with the branches they extend from their hidden boles. Salal, ferns, and deadfall, which are part of the ground between, are cast in shadow minimally dappled with light. Forty feet from me the sun shines full on a large expanse of huckleberry that fills an opening between my trees and the alders that crowd the spaces on the other side of that brief clearing. I know that a walking path lies through that light, on the other side of the huckleberry but I cannot see it, nor anyone who walks that way.

When I first stepped into this little 107 square foot cabin, unplumbed, unheated except for a small cast iron wood stove, I was enveloped, through the heat and humid closeness of this unusually warm summer, by the slightly oppressive smells of still new paint and raw wood. Although I hear the flight path far overhead, birdsong and raven's caw, the barely perceptible buzz of hidden insects, and the tapping of the keys on my keyboard or the scratch of my pen on the paper, stillness and silence surround me. Sitting here, wrapped in these sensory impressions, I am filled with as many different feelings as I am by sights, smells, and sounds. I feel at first awe, anticipation, and hope. These are the first feelings I remember and which I still feel first, even now, as I experience this place finally realized.

As noted in my introduction, I had long held a vision for a contemplative Christian retreat center. Through mutual friends I met Kathi Bentall who became my ministry placement supervisor at the Listening Post. We often had time to talk and vision during quiet periods or on our walk home together, back to the nearby neighborhood where we both lived.

During one of these quiet spaces I shared my vision of creating a retreat center and discovered that she had held a similar vision for many years, and the land to realize it for the past seven. We were both filled with awe and the stirrings of hopeful anticipation that we tried to restrain with reminders of the many real barriers that were between us and the fulfillment of the vision. "What is God doing here, bringing us together, at this time with this common vision?", we couldn't help but ask. I had written my vision out in the form of a proposal and Kathi asked to see it. When I brought it to her our talk began in earnest about her vision and the hermitage land (lot 2448) which Wolfgang Duntz had zoned and agreed to donate for a retreat center on a second site at the south end of Bowen.

Although a small group of visionaries had created a model of the envisioned hermitage community, renovating and furnishing two cabins on the land, the site was not developed as it was hoped to be and could be used only minimally until the property was subdivided. As visioning progressed, many complications arose. Wolfgang wrote to Kathi and Shirley about the Cowan Point property: "If you are not scared by now (having read about the many challenges to starting Rivendell on the Cates Hill property), then please read my letter abut Cowan Point. In comparison with Cowan Point, Cates Hill is an example of simplicity."[1] While Kathi waited she tried working with other local organizations to develop a retreat center with the vision of the second site but nothing worked. Three years after the first hermitage conversation Kathi and I had, we had developed our friendship and learned to wait through the roadblocks that kept coming between us and realizing our vision.

Braxton Hicks

Then suddenly it seemed as though labor pains were beginning. The landlord sold the house in which my family and I were tenants and the Hawthorne Foundation agreed to financially support the project. Kathi suggested that we consider moving to Bowen Island in order to be near the hermitage land, readied to begin development. Her brother's carriage house was available and he and his wife agreed to rent it to us although they had been previously reluctant to take in tenants. In the whirl of the sudden upheaval my husband and I met with a clearness committee of our friends in the Quaker

1 excerpt from a letter from Wolfgang Duntz to Shirley, Howard, and Kathi Bentall, March 15, 2001.

style presented by Parker Palmer. There was general agreement that moving to Bowen Island seemed to be the next step for us.

We involved our children in the decision, giving them one week to listen to God on their own and ask of us any questions they had. We then gathered as a family to share what we each felt we had heard from God. At the end of the week we discovered we were in complete agreement to make the move. Seeing my children seriously listening to God, raising insightful questions, and fully participating in our discernment process, was one of the gifts of awe and wonder that moved me during this time.

At the end of June we moved to Bowen Island to live near lot 2448, the original hermitage site.[2] I took responsibility for bookings and welcomed new retreatants to the little two cabin site As a family we shared in the care-taking needs. Soon after the move we also became involved with the Rivendell Lodge community, helping out with basic tasks such as setting up rooms, washing and folding laundry, and eventually substitute hosting. After our move the hermitage became used more regularly and the desire to develop Lot 2448 increased. It became apparent, however, that this was not going to happen as smoothly as we had anticipated at our clearness committee. Conflicting interests and a general lack of energy for the Hermitage vision by the funding body prevented any development and we sat on Bowen Island waiting with waning hope. As we watched the dead leaves of our second autumn on Bowen fall to the ground we also watched fall our final hopes for the Hermitage site. Kathi and I were both struggling with discouragement.

One day, as I was sitting beside the stream that flows past the edge of the yard and praying, I was reminded of Elijah. The stream I sat beside was also a wadi in a ravine and ravens abide there as well. I felt that I, like Elijah, was sitting by a wadi that was drying up in the drought of political fractions and that the hopes we had moved on were drying up like the wadi. I felt only the hope and

2. Thanks to Brendan and Julie Morey who let us stay with them between our June 25th, 2011 moving date and July 1st, 2011 so that Dave could finish his teaching year before we moved to Bowen Island.

promise of the ravens and the widow—God's continued care for us in the midst.

Unknown to me, Kathi had a similar experience. On that same Saturday she attended an Eastside StoryGuild[3] presentation on the story of Abraham and Lot. The writers and directors, Tama Ward Balisky and Carsten Crolow, had originally planned to act Abraham as pious, but instead chose him to be vulnerable. Abraham's human vulnerability deeply impacted Kathi and she felt that she was invited to release the best land to "Lot," receiving for "herself" what remained. She called me when she got home.

I could hear the concern in her voice over the phone and felt concerned myself at what I had to tell her about my experience by the stream. Dave and I agreed to meet her. We met at the Rivendell lodge, feeling that this was the end of the vision we had held for so many years. We sat down on the couches and looked at each other, neither wanting to let the other down. Kathi started, "I am so sorry to have to tell you both this, but I have had an experience through the Storyguild presentation and I believe that I am to release the present partnership with Hawthorne and let the land, lot 2448, revert back to Wolfgang." She shared her full experience with us. I don't know what she expected but I think she was surprised when we responded with relief rather than dismay. With more awe than discouragement, I shared with Kathi my vision of Elijah by the wadi and we both rested in the shared guidance we had received. We mutually agreed that the only thing to do was to let the land go. We had no idea when we made this decision that it would have better consequences than we could have anticipated.

Kathi talked to Wolfgang when she got back from her silent retreat. To our surprise he offered to exchange the land Kathi was relinquishing for one of two other sites. Wolfgang walked with us over the two new sites and we agreed that lot 1411 seemed the

---

3 "Eastside Story Guild is a performing arts initiative that works with children, youth, and adult mentors to tell biblical stories using world arts, drama, and music for the purpose of nurturing confidence and hope in young people, stewarding cultural heritage, and promoting spiritual awareness in the public sphere." *ESG mission statement, thanks to Tama Ward Balisky of Sacred Canopy Productions.*

most promising. Kathi released lot 2448 and tentatively acquired lot 1411 which was better for the purpose of silence, insurance costs, and property taxes. While it did not have the beautiful ocean frontage of the first lot the intimacy of the woods invited one inward. It was also easier and more affordable to build on and more accessible for walking trails.

Kathi continued her discernment on her annual extended silent retreat. During the same period I too went on silent retreat for continued discernment, though mine was enforced. I had no voice from December 23rd until the end of February while recovering from thyroid surgery. During my enforced silent retreat I walked the land and spent time in prayer trying to come to a place of peace and detachment in the midst of all the changes, releasing to God my hopes for the development and the uncertainty around the impending decisions. As we celebrated Christ's conception and birth, my thoughts were full of the pregnancy of this place and hope for new life.

When I met with Kathi after this month of discernment and prayer, our decision to develop a silent retreat space on lot 1411 was confirmed. Kathi had a particular investment set aside and held by FOCA[4], a non profit organization she closed, donating the funds to the Rivendell Foundation for the development of a hermitage site. She approached the Hawthorne Foundation once again, this time to apply for a matched donation. They agreed to match Kathi's donation and further, committed to the completion of the main house. We were ready to begin the development on the new site which, now unencumbered by complications, could start immediately. We decided to form a visioning committee and invited those we thought suited. We also invited anyone from the Rivendell lodge hosting community who was experienced in silence and held a particular interest in this vision for the second site. Thus began a year of preparation.

---

4. FOCA - Fuente (Fountain) of Contemplation and Action was formed when lot 2448 was set aside for the development of the second site. However, as a non profit it was not able to serve as an operating body for the foundation.

VII.

The Hermitage: Realizing the Vision

Afte ten years of holding the vision for the second site, the most significant obstacles to the third phase of the Rivendell development were finally cleared away and we were ready to begin. As it had been held so it was renewed—by vision. Kathi sent this letter to those whom we invited to be part of the visioning group:

> Hi Everyone,
>
> As I think all of you are aware, since the very early days of Rivendell I have had the vision of an additional site that would be dedicated to silence with individual cabins that are simple and nestled in nature. The property called The Hermitage down by Seymour Bay was acquired with this purpose in mind. Through what has been a long process, the property has been released from that commitment. However, another piece of land has now been made available. It is on the other end of the golf course from Seymour Bay and appears to be more suited to our purpose. The intention is that the site will be donated to Rivendell Foundation and the operations would come under the society's jurisdiction.
>
> Jennifer Graves (who has just joined the society's board) and I are working together to bring this vision to reality. We would like to gather a group of people to vision together. We plan to begin with one day of

discussion and then collectively decide on a planning process. We wanted to invite any of you who might have a particular interest is this vision that is rooted in your own experience in silent retreat or with other similar retreat centers. Please let us know if you would like to be included in this initial meeting.

Blessings,

Kathi

We held the first visioning meeting on April 9th, 2012—Easter Monday, and celebrated Rivendell's Tenth Anniversary on June 3, 2012. From that first meeting a smaller visioning team was formed of people who were willing to commit to more frequent meetings. The second site finally had its steering committee!

The visioning focus group met through the spring and summer to clarify the unique mandate of the Second Site. We agreed that the new development, now called the Rivendell Hermitage, would embrace Rivendell's mission statement, identifying itself with the addendum, "The Hermitage is a site particularly dedicated to individuals, silence, and solitude." We also developed a unique set of six principles that reflected its unique mandate in the overall vision of the Rivendell Retreat Center. In the fall and winter of 2012 and 2013, with the vision and principles guiding the planning, Kathi and I met alternately with the visioning committee and with Don Nicholson and Barbara Whaler to design the main house and apply for a building permit. I recalled Shirley's journal of Rivendell's first development when she mentions, "lawyers, lawyers, and more lawyers!" and thought, "permits, permits, and more permits!" Driveway permits, sewage permits, building permits, and occupancy permits—all had forms to fill in, requirements to fulfill, and long periods of waiting, often having to get more information, other approvals, or wait for something to be completed before we could receive our much needed, long awaited, permits.

Prayers and Paths

At the very beginning of the year of preparation, when we had decided to switch the lands I began walking the land, tending the space with prayer each Saturday throughout this period of planning. When I first walked through the land, I was impressed by the abundance of life, old and new, that surrounded us. The longer I walked the land the more I noticed: the young nurse trees such as the Alder and Hemlock, and those stalwarts of more ancient days: Douglas Fir, Cedars, and wonder of wonders, even a 400 year old Pacific Yew! I noticed new grasses naturally restoring old but still walkable logging paths. These were the most accessible places and so the first discovered. Living things filled the forest: Wrens, Towhees, Finches, Robins, Pileated Woodpeckers and their smaller Sapsucker relatives, are just some of the many birds I heard or saw. Deer had made their beds under large old trees for many years while other smaller and more fragile creatures, such as insects, frogs, and salamanders had laid their eggs near the creek and on old, decaying logs. And all around the silence was deep and still and inward.

As I went increasingly deeper into thick, untouched areas, the rocky landscape was covered with tall trees and foxglove, rotting logs and thistle, spreading salal and ferns, all of which created a nearly impassable yet beautiful undergrowth. The trees reached high over my head as I "lifted my eyes to heaven" and saw the canopied sky. I wonder if Jesus, when he "lifted his eyes to heaven" before he prayed, was met with any such wonders in his desert surroundings, or if the sky itself was beautiful in its vastness. These days of prayer remain some of my most precious memories of the development. The land was still reclaiming its wildness and I felt a permitted intruder. All of creation around me spoke of the glory of God in the hidden places of the world, in the unknown retreatants who would make their pilgrimage here, and of my own unknown silent soul.

The Hermitage land is shaped roughly like a south pointing triangle, bordered along one side by the year-round Josephine Creek, a gently used road on the other, and along the bottom private property with a portion of designated parkland. When the visioning committee met for the first time on Easter Monday we introduced them to the contours and shape of the site and spent a few hours in the afternoon walking or sitting on the land in solitary silence and prayer. The darkness created by the vast overshadowing trees and the fallen trunks and dense undergrowth made it difficult to walk the land and invited us to create gentle, meandering paths.

In May a group of high school students[1] came and created our first trail from the entrance of the land to the ancient Yew tree that stood at the opening of a circle of old cedars—a place that had come to feel especially sacred to us.

We received our driveway permit on Oct. 10, 2013 and began clearing for it soon after. I was amazed at what a difference a driveway and a walking trail make! Suddenly the forest I had slowly stumbled over was open and easily accessed. The site seemed much smaller than it had when it took me two or more hours to make my way from one side of the lot to the other!

Construction Days

Building the House

On November 2nd, 2013 we held the ground breaking and finally, after much long waiting, on November 6th we received our building permit and site preparations began. The early part of building was very slow and complicated compared to our expectations. The site was unserviced. Since we wanted to keep our environmental footprint as small as possible, choosing responsible power and water sources became a consuming concern. In the end we decided to connect with hydro and access our water from the stream using the water license attached to the property. Unfortunately, this plan for our water resulted in unforeseen complications and a two year

---

1. The first of several groups of teenagers from West Coast Christian Secondary School from Vancouver, BC, Canada that came throughout the years of development and who are responsible for many of the trails on the Hermitage site.

process of working on an agreement with the neighbors. We finally decided to hook up with the local utility.

We had to blast a larger area for the house than we were prepared for, the foundation was larger than anticipated, the septic field needed costly work, and site preparation costs continued to escalate and take far more time than we had expected. Finally, after waiting three months for the site to be readied for building, Kathi's nephew, Cody Bentall[2] and crew began building. While we waited for site preparations I created a blog to tell the story of the progress of our development as it unfolded.[3] As I kept the story going on the blog I noted, "The building goes up so fast I can barely keep track of all the changes." Cody and company began building on January 16th, 2014 and the metal roof went up on March 25th. The inside of the building was finished in early June. We had an effective temporary water solution but were still waiting for hydro. Finally, on July 30th we received our hydro connection and could apply for our occupancy permit.

2. Founder and owner of High Bar Construction, previously doing business as Bentall Taylor Construction.

3. This blog has become our website and can be accessed at *www.hermitage.rivendellretreat.org*.

Raising the Shelters

On August 9th, 2014 we began to host a series of weekend teams to build three individual sleeping shelters. Two shelters were funded by the Sisters of St. Anne and one was funded by generous donations from members of the Anglican parish, St. Francis of Assisi[4]. There was great excitement in the air as we began to build. From the very beginning of our visioning we had wanted to build the cabins with volunteer labor. On the one hand it was, theoretically, a cost-saving choice, but more importantly it was in keeping with our vision of soul hospitality and simplicity. We wanted the Hermitage developed by a community of people, not just one individual or company.

As the time approached Kathi recommended we hire Thomas Dickau, whom we had both known for several years, to oversee the teams of volunteers and the building of the shelters. Thomas was about to complete his carpentry apprenticeship and had already participated in local building projects, many with a social justice component. He was personable, reliable and a proven team builder and leader. I felt excited when Kathi suggested Thomas to me. She connected with him and he agreed to lead the building teams of volunteers to build three sleeping shelters the first year and two more the year after.[5]

The teams came and brought volunteer cooks and sleeping mats with them. We paid for their transportation and their food and they slept in the main house on their mats.

The first team prepared each shelter site, set the cement foundation blocks in position, and built the wooden platforms upon which each hermitage cabin rests. The second weekend a men's home group from Grandview Calvary Baptist Church worked far

4. St. Francis of Assisi has been a generous contributor to our project not only through financial donations but also through the gifts of second-hand furniture, lamps, etc. needed for the house and cabins.

5 We originally planned for nine shelters plus a gate keeper cabin giving a capacity of 12 but as we became more familiar with the land and the capacity of the main house, we realized that a community of twelve was too large to retain an ambiance of solitude. We decided that the vision was more important than the extra income generated by doubling our capacity and losing the gifts of spaciousness and silence that draw us to God.

harder than they had anticipated to carry hundreds of pounds of SIPs[6] to the sites and begin raising the walls and roof. A few teachers, including my husband and a friend visiting from Vancouver Island, came by after the shelter raising weekend to put on the roof of the second shelter and raise the walls and roof of the third. We began each weekend with a short reading of a Bible passage and praying together from a liturgical prayer I wrote[7]. We hoped to build the shelters as an embodied form of prayer.

The walls and roofs were up and ready when the next team, a mixed group of all ages, arrived to put on the siding, the roofing, and install the windows. There was a job for everyone. My daughters helped Thomas put on the roofing of the second cabin and joined other children and adults in the afternoon to put up cedar siding. Adults of all ages worked side by side installing windows, measuring the wood, the walls, and the window frames, and participating in whatever work was necessary to make sure the building was done well and safely. On Labor Day weekend and the week following we painted the interior walls. The following weekend the wood stoves were installed, the interior ceilings paneled, and laminate flooring completed in each shelter. The following weekends until October saw Thomas alone or with small teams finishing off final details. In October we brought in the furniture and prepared the cabins for retreatants.

Three shelters were thus completed by the end of October but because of difficulties getting enough water pressure from our temporary system, we had not yet received our occupancy permit. By November we had begun to receive hydro bills and have the increased expenses of running a large house without any income. In the meantime I continued to work with Wan Phek How[8] to choose and tailor the booking system he created for us. We also turned my blog into a website that retained important pieces of the

6. SIPs stands for "structurally insulated panels" and is a pre-fabricated fully finished wall or roof with styrofoam insulation.

7. These liturgies can be found in the appendix.

8. Wan Phek How, founder and owner of Rojak Systems, also created the booking system for the Rivendell Lodge.

Hermitage story for those following the development on the blog while also including information geared to retreatants. We were able to welcome the first retreatants to the Hermitage in January.

Opening Days

The early days were perhaps the busiest time of the development—for me, anyway—Kathi, who was deeply involved with neighbors and permits, may feel otherwise. With bills coming in, retreatants regularly emailing with retreat requests, and the house and shelters standing empty though ready, we were growing impatient to receive our occupancy permit. In November and December Kathi and I along with other members of the visioning committee spent much of our time at the Hermitage. We sewed curtains, found needs and filled them, cut up magazines as art materials, set-up the prayer loft, the kitchen, the bedrooms, and the sleeping shelters. We lit the stoves and wrote up how to do so safely for retreatants. We wrote and revised a hosting binder, orientation sheets, welcome sheets, to-do lists, housekeeping checklists, emergency contacts, sewage guidelines, and posted notices about thermostat operation and fireplace safety. We restrained ourselves from going overboard and kept the main house out of a Richard Scarry book. I began booking people for January when we were told that was when we would likely receive our occupancy permit.

In January everything began to pick up speed. I barely remember this period with much clarity or reality. We received our occupancy permit and were hosting retreatants but we still did not have a fully functioning hosting community. We were filled with excitement at opening but were also concerned over mounting bills. Would we have enough retreatants to cover expenses even without a mortgage or staff? Kathi and I had sat down together and set up a tentative budget but as real expenses continued to pour in we continued to revise our budget and make our explanations to the Society board. With tensions mounting, Rita Krana- better opened the journal she kept from the founding days of the Rivendell Lodge and read an entry bemoaning unexpected costs, difficulties predicting the budget for a yet untried project, and the concern that the Lodge would not receive enough retreatants to cover the real budget. Hearing that the Lodge had also struggled with financial uncertainty and knowing it had made it successfully through its early days was very encouraging!

Throughout our first year of operations I have experienced what the founders and members of the hosting community of the Rivendell Lodge had repeatedly told me while I was listening to their stories of the first development: the full importance of starting a retreat center without any debt or financial encumbrances! Even several months into operations we could not have continued to operate out of our socially radical principle of accessibility if we had an outstanding mortgage or salaries to pay.

Although it was only slightly more than a month before we had somewhat regular on-site hosts, this period felt very long. I had agreed to serve as an off site host when we had retreatants but no host on site. Initially this was a frequent occurrence. Some of the visioning committee had chosen to serve as hosts for the Hermitage but we had thirty days to fill every month and only a few hosts taking a few days. I was thankful for each day of every host!

I was also the primary person responsible for bookings and communications with retreatants at this time. By the beginning of February I was feeling quite stretched. My friend Wai Mei, hearing how tired I was feeling, shared a story by Evy Klassen, from a book written by her and her husband Steve, directors and founders of the Mark Center in Abbotsford, British Columbia, Canada.[9] When the Mark Center was completed and beginning to welcome retreatants Evy realized she was exhausted—at the worst possible time! The energy they had spent developing the space had taken what they now needed to host the space. She wanted to quit. I could relate. As she wrote her story, she reflected that after creation, just like after birth, there is a much needed time of rest. Unfortunately, when there is a new baby in the house, few people get a good night's sleep![10]

9. Klassen, *Your Ears Will Hear*, 138.

10. I created the birth analogy from her reference to needing a rest after the

At the same time, Kathi, whose time was filled to overflowing with many other needs of the Hermitage, was also feeling the burden of opening days and felt like she was carrying everything by herself. We both were reluctant to lay our burdens on the other since we knew that the other carried many responsibilities of her own. When we finally shared our mutual feeling of being overwhelmed by waves of the new responsibilities washing over us, Kathi recalled that she and her mother had experienced similar tumult and stress when opening the Lodge. We recognized that this stage of development could lead us to conflict or clearer communication. I feel that we were able to communicate more clearly, name our need to find others who could share some of the tasks, and find ways to name what we each were carrying.

On Wai Mei's urging, at the next hosting community meeting I brought forth the demands of off-site hosting and invited the whole community to consider greater sharing of the hosting needs. The shift from feeling I had to carry it by myself to feeling that I could share the load with others, and seeing them wholeheartedly receive the invitation, brought me much freedom in my role at the Hermitage. Kathi also discovered one woman, Marguerite Wahl, who was interested in becoming more involved and we invited her to consider taking over the booking system since she showed real aptitude in this area. Marguerite agreed.

This has been so successful that I now have very few hosting duties or booking responsibilities and Kathi and I have more energy to invest in other areas. For example, we are currently considering offering, with others, regular silent retreats for retreatants desiring a guided introduction to the practices of solitude and silence at the Hermitage. The sharing of Hermitage responsibilities was also timely for Kathi as she was required to take on greater responsibilities at the Lodge during the transition time between some of the original hosts stepping back and experiencing the full effects of the efforts of the succession committee.

---

creation is completed.

Enfleshing and Sustaining the Vision:
The Hermitage Hosting Community

Hosting at the Hermitage site is very different than at the Lodge. Hermitage hosts welcome retreatants when they arrive and orient them to the site. They also orient them to what it means to practice silence and solitude in community. If there is an emergency, the hosts know who to contact and how. However, because the practice of solitude and silence are new or unfamiliar spiritual disciplines to many,[11] the primary responsibility of the hosts of the Hermitage is to demonstrate through their own practice what the expression of solitude and silence is like in the experience of this retreat community. They also hold the eight o'clock centering prayer time and lead the evening five o'clock worship which is held with more silence than during the Lodge five o'clock gathering. To reflect the unique focus of Rivendell's second site, the evening offering is guided lectio divina which begins with 20 minutes of silence.

Spiritual Direction is also available to all retreatants and hosts who are qualified to offer spiritual direction may do so. If a host is not qualified then Kathi or I make arrangements to meet with the retreatants that request accompaniment.[12]

Retreatants at the Hermitage are asked to take even greater involvement in the care of the retreat space than at the Lodge. They bring their own food and bedding in and out with them and clean their own and shared spaces so that they leave the place ready to

11. cf Foster, Richard J. 1998. *Celebration of Discipline: The Path to Spiritual Growth.* USA: HarperCollins, ch. 7 for an introduction to these practices in mainstream Christian practice. For a more extended, focused introduction cf Martin Laird. 2006. *Into the Silent Land: A Guide to the Christian Practice of Contemplation.* New York: Oxford University Press.

12 As the Hermitage was approaching readiness and the visioning committee deciding on the qualifications of hosts it became apparent that it was time for me to become qualified in spiritual direction. As the building was going up I enrolled in the Art of Spiritual Direction with SoulStream which was offered from Abbotsford, BC. As Kathi and I were realizing the importance of this step she remembered that she and Margaret McAvity received their qualifications through the Mercy Center in California around this same time in the development of the lodge: Kathi in 1996 and Margaret after Rivendell started. Spiritual direction is available at both Rivendell sites.

welcome the next retreatant. Hosts are not expected to do any cleaning or care taking beyond what would be expected of any other retreatant. While all work is held as the work of prayer here as at the Lodge, the unique emphasis of the Hermitage invites a greater sharing of the work so that hosts can model the practice of solitude and silence for retreatants and bring greater intentionality to facilitating its unique ambiance.

Conclusion

As I prepare this book for publication, teams of volunteers, once again under the direction of Thomas Dickau, are building two more sleeping shelters. This will give us space for seven retreatants at the Hermitage, including the host. Seven people may not be quite as isolated as one expects when one hears the word "hermitage" and yet the nature of this space seems to make a sense of community and solitude possible with this many.

We hold a vision of creating a separate sanctuary next year, perhaps hand built with cob, and an outdoor sanctuary around the circle of cedars by the old Yew tree, but this part of the story has not even reached the preparation, planning, or fund-raising stage, and I remember—the Rivendell sanctuary took ten years to be re-alized. And so, in the end, there is no end, only more beginnings. In a culture characterized by rushed and shallow living, growing dissatisfaction with the church, and a longing for deep, authentic spirituality, perhaps places such as Rivendell Lodge or Rivendell Hermitage can offer space where people can slow down and attend to their spiritual longings and needs, with their roots in Jesus, their empowerment in the Spirit, and their beginnings in the great story that embraces us all and draws us into the mystery which is God.

Appendix A

*The Original Vision for a Retreat Centre
on Cates Hill, Bowen Island*

Our Vision is that Rivendell will become a place where people, especially those who have limited resources and special needs, will be able to come for quietness, reflection and spiritual renewal or growth. We hope that its inspiring natural setting and proximity to Vancouver will help to draw people, young and old, to opportunities for pausing for new perspectives and a deepening of faith along the journey of life.

*Basic Principles that we have been working with
in the early stages of the planning:*

1. *Accessibility for People with Limited Resources:* Many facilities exist for those who can afford them but there is a shortage of places for people with limited resources. The content challenge of Jesus was to journey with people who are marginalized and excluded from dominant society.

2. *The Virtue of Simplicity:* In keeping with those who will be using it and the Christian challenge to the opulence of our time, we hope to set up the retreat centre in a style of comfort but simplicity.

3. *Quietude/Silence:* In a culture of words and distractions, there is hunger for a place to be still and listen for the presence of God. Our overall vision includes the hope of a second site where small, silent retreats may be held, offering the profound spiritual experience that is available to people searching for God in the simplicity of silence. In the meantime, the attic of the lodge has been designed with the expectation that it may sometimes be used for this purpose and our hope its that Rivendell, generally, will be a place where people may find quietness and an inner experience of peace.

4. *Stewardship of Resources/Environmental Responsibility:* In this day of scarce resources and so much need around the world we are called to be stewards of what we have. We will hope to apply this principle in the purchasing and use of supplies, in recycling, composting, etc. and encouraging a simple, not wasteful, style of living.

5. *Access to Nature:* Our natural world is an expression of the handiwork of the Creator. It is not surprising that people on retreat discover intimacy with God in nature. Our sense, as we wander forest paths, are in themselves a pathway to God. The retreat centre will provide ready access to nature and foster respect for the environment.

6. *Spirit of Openness:* While the centre is rooted in Christianity it will be spent o people of other faiths and to those who have no acknowledged faith, with the hope that it will provide a deepening experience for them as they journey through life.

Long-term, the retreat centre will be responsible to the board of directors of Rivendell Society, which has now been incorporated but is not yet functioning. In the short term, we welcome the Steering Committee to provide valuable insights and help in much of the decision-making through the months of planning, praying, construction, furnishing, and organizing. *Thank you for being willing to join with us in steering through these first essential stages of bringing our vision for Rivendell Retreat into reality.*

Howard, Shirley, and Kathi Bentall
September 15, 2001.

Appendix B

The Rivendell Retreat Community Covenant

Rivendell Community members as followers of Christ, responding to a sense of call, are invited by Rivendell Retreat Society's Board of Directors to steward the daily life of Rivendell.

The purpose of this community is to be open to the leading of God's Spirit in the unfolding vision of Rivendell, embracing a ministry of hospitality and discerning ongoing ways of caring for this sacred place and for those who come.

In covenanting together . . .

1. We commit ourselves to pray for the life of Rivendell and for each other.

2. We are committed to our own spiritual growth and we endeavour to make a personal retreat each year.

3. We endeavour to be present at 3 community retreats yearly, at work weeks and other community events.

4. We commit ourselves to accept responsibilities for the harmonious and efficient functioning of our evolving life at Rivendell as we are able and according to our gifts.

Although our amount of hosting service at Rivendell varies considerably, each of us recognizes that it is this service which ultimately binds us, and it is the one for which we are most accountable.

1. In our hosting service at Rivendell we commit ourselves humbly to be the "arms of Jesus"; welcoming and being attentive to the wellbeing of all who come here. We take responsibility for the daily 8 a.m. and 5 p.m. sacred times. According to our gifts, we are available for prayer, spiritual companioning and retreat leadership.

2. While hosting at Rivendell, we take responsibility for bookings, for quality control in housekeeping, and for the general security and well being of the buildings and property. We commit ourselves normally to have 2 hosts on watch at Rivendell, and at all times we will have someone accessible.

3. We honor each other's varied commitments, trusting that others in the community are available to be present as hosts in our absence.

4. In transferring hosting responsibilities, every effort will be made to have an adequate changeover time for the purpose of being clear about present Rivendell realities and to connect as community.

As the Rivendell Community . . .

1. We are committed to being a diverse community of Christians open to being challenged, encouraged and admonished in order to build us up as fuller members of the Body of Christ. In our relationships with each other we seek a spirit of openness, honesty and transparency, being Christ to and with each other.

2. Our stewardship ministry to Rivendell is voluntary in nature.

3. We honour those who are in the process of discernment for community membership, occasional watchkeeping and eldership.

4. We are part of the larger family of Rivendell, including circles of elders, watchkeepers, volunteers and a larger circle of thousands who have been here to experience retreat.

We commit ourselves to review our covenant regularly, desiring to be open to God's Spirit, both as individuals and community, for we are conscious of not wanting to be limited with a "written" covenant.

January, 2004
Revised December 2006
Revised January 2008
Revised September 2014

Appendix C

Circles of Community Life: Diagram

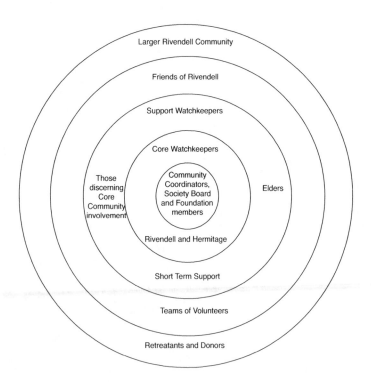

Larger Rivendell Community

Friends of Rivendell

Support Watchkeepers

Core Watchkeepers

Those discerning Core Community involvement

Community Coordinators, Society Board and Foundation members

Elders

Rivendell and Hermitage

Short Term Support

Teams of Volunteers

Retreatants and Donors

Circles of Community Life: Description

1. *Coordination and Leadership*

   - We will continue the practice of naming Co-Coordinators for six-month terms from the Core Watch Keeper. We will be intentional in mentoring new coordinators with the less experienced coordinator taking a lead role in the second half of the six month term.

   - The main decision-making group is the Core Community.

   - This group meets three times a year at retreats and in maintenance week if necessary.

   - Co-Coordinators attend the Rivendell Society meetings, giving reports and bringing forward items requiring policy decisions.

   - Spokespersons for Rivendell are one of the current co-ordinators and/or the Chair of the Board.

2. *Core Watch Keepers*

   a. *Lodge*

   - Membership in this circle includes a commitment of and average of at least five days a month of Watch Keeping at Rivendell throughout the year.

   - We honor one another's varying commitments in other parts of our lives.

   - In addition to this monthly commitment, Core Watch Keepers will attend community retreats.

   - Core Watch Keepers will demonstrate an energy and ability to carry out duties typical of this circle.

   - The days of participation and hosting/facilitating during Christmas and Easter retreats is to be included in the monthly commitment of time.

b. *Hermitage Watch Keepers*

- Membership in this circle also includes a commitment of an average of at least five days a month of Watch Keeping throughout the year.

- We honor one another's varying commitments in other parts of our lives.

- Core Watch Keepers will demonstrate an energy and ability to carry out duties typical of this circle.

- Participation in the Rivendell community retreats is yet to be determined and will depend on the theme of the retreat.

3. *Support Watch Keepers including discerners and elders:*

- Membership in this circle includes commitment of consistent and flexible involvement in the Watch Keeping life of Rivendell. A number of days a month is not specified.

- This involvement provides a point of entry into the Community and movement toward eldership.

- Support Watch Keepers are encouraged to attend Community retreats and maintenance weeks.

- As community members transition from active watch keeping to eldership, they are welcome to be a continuing presence at Rivendell either alongside other watch keepers or availing themselves of Rivendell for their own retreat times. They are welcome to attend community retreats as appropriate.

4. *Friends of Rivendell—Teams of Volunteers*

- We identify two kinds of tasks: a) regular, recurring, routine and b)occasional

- The regular, routine, and recurring Tasks (Aspects of Service) that we agree could be taken on by other volunteers: recycling, gardening, carpentry, 5 o'clock worship, maintenance work, support during change-over, labyrinth care, monitoring supplies, spiritual accompaniment, sewing, transportation

- Identify a coordinator to organize this level of volunteer involvement

- Respect areas of vested interest and special interest

- To access and strengthen relationships with the wider volunteer retreat community we need to address communications issues and organize information sharing times

5. *Retreatants and Financial Donors*

   Retreats and Spiritual Companioning
   for the Circles of Community

   1. Community Retreats and work weeks

      - There will continue to be three retreats a year: January, June, and September

      - There will be two work weeks: five days in the spring, and three days in the fall

   2. Focus of the Retreats

      - One retreat will focus on spiritual companionship: process, practice, and preparation with leadership of internal or external facilitator(s) *[attendance: Core and Support Watch Keepers, Elders, and select Volunteers from Lodge and Hermitage]*

      - One retreat, with external leadership, will feed our souls, developing our spirituality, and drawing on diverse media such as music and art *[attendance: Core and Support Watch Keepers, Volunteers from Lodge and Hermitage, and Board members]*

      - One retreat will be functional, addressing planning, Watch Keeping issues, training of community members, and other practical matters related to Rivendell operations (could be at same time as AGM) *[attendance: Core and Support Watch Keepers only]*

3. Concerning Work Weeks

   • Attendance at Work Weeks is optional and includes all the Circles of Support

   • A business-oriented meeting might be held in the context of Work Week

4. Spiritual Accompaniment defined

   • 'Spiritual Companioning' refers to a time of sacred listening with any guest who wants to be heard while they are at Rivendell.

   • 'Spiritual Direction' refers to *an ongoing relationship* of spiritual accompaniment

Readings and Prayers for the Building of the Hermitages

for Establishing the Foundations

One: As we come together to prepare the shelters for those who come here looking for rest, respite, and connection with the Holy One, we pray for them, that they may feel the embrace of your love as they are embraced by these shelters and this place, a living sanctuary.

All: May the work of our hands and the meditation of our hearts be pleasing to you, O Lord.

One: As we clear the spaces for these shelters, we pray for those who come here to find spaciousness within themselves. We pray that they may clear the clutter within so that the soil of their hearts is ready to make room for you.

All: May the work of our hands and the meditation of our hearts be pleasing to you, O Lord.

One: As we orient the shelters, we pray for those who come here to find the direction they need to orient their lives back to the Centre which sometimes gets lost or confused in the busyness and distractions of the many demands in our daily lives.

All: May the work of our hands and the meditation of our hearts be pleasing to you, O Lord.

One: As we lay the concrete cornerstones, build the foundation, and lay the floor, we pray for all who come here, that they may find you deep within, the true cornerstone and foundation, to support their journey into healing and spiritual renewal.

All: May the work of our hands and the meditation of our hearts be pleasing to you, O Lord.

for Raising the Walls and Installing the Windows
(*Optional Reading*) Psalm 27

One: As we come together to raise walls assembled by others upon foundations that were prepared by builders who went before us, we pray for those who will come after us, to build and to rest. May they know that they are not alone. May they experience the shelter of being held by a larger community of those who have gone before and those who will come after.

All: May the work of our hands and the meditation of our hearts be pleasing to you, O Lord.

One: As we raise these shelters we pray for those who will take shelter in them. May they know the comfort, security, and healing that comes from knowing oneself sheltered in your love. May this sheltering space point to the sheltering space within and the sheltering arms of God that surround them.

All: May the work of our hands and the meditation of our hearts be pleasing to you, O Lord.

One: As we install the windows we pray for those who will be blessed by them. As they sit in rays of sun or moon streaming through them we pray that they may know the rays of your love shining on them. As they listen to the rain, we pray that they may they experience the rain of your love falling over them. Or as they see through the clear glass to the beauty of your creation, or with eyes turned inward, we pray that this may be a thin space between the temporary and the eternal.

All: May the work of our hands and the meditation of our hearts be pleasing to you, O Lord.

for the Siding and Roofing
(*Optional Reading*) Isaiah 25

One: O LORD, as we come together to build these shelters, fulfilling plans for this place formed long ago, we pray for those who will come here longing for the fulfillment of the plans for them that you have formed long ago. We pray that they may know the joy of joining with you to live into the faithful and sure plans you have for them. We join with those who have gone behind and those who go before us, praising your name for the wonderful things you have done and the wonderful things you will do. And as we prepare for this day of work, we take time to enter, as they will, into the prayerful silence that is here. (*silence*)

All: May the work of our hands and the meditation of our hearts be pleasing to you, O LORD.

One: As we wrap each shelter with cedar siding, we pray for those you come here, that they would be wrapped in your protective love. May these shelters which we are building be a place of refuge for the needy, the poor, and all those in distress. (*silence*)

All: May the work of our hands and the meditation of our hearts be pleasing to you, O LORD.

One: As we cover the shelter with roofing to shield these shelters from the elements, we pray for those who will come here longing to be shielded from the elements that beat against them in their daily lives. We pray that as they find refuge under this roof they may they find refuge under the shelter of your wings. (Ps. 61:4) (*silence*)

All: May the work of our hands and the meditation of our hearts be pleasing to you, O LORD.

One: May your hand rest on this place, O LORD.

All: Amen

Bibliography

Doherty, Catherine de Hueck. *Poustinia: Christian Spirituality of the East for Western Man*. Notre Dame, Ind.: Ave Maria, 1975.

Klassen, Steve and Ely Klassen. *Your Ears Will Hear: A Journal for Listening to God*. Abbotsford, BC: Mark Centre in association with Namesake Writing Services and Relevention Marketing, Inc., 2011.